This workbook contains material from many sources, which include:

Carl Casanova, M.S.
Articles from the Internet
and the belief that there is no such thing as an original thought – everything that you will learn in this workbook – you already knew – this is just a refresher!

All materials contained in this workbook are proprietary and are not to be duplicated (unless worksheets for your work) or used for any purpose other than personal without written permission from Judith Auslander of Wise Heart Coaching. Thank you.

Copyright © 2008 Wise Heart Coaching
Revised 2012 and 2014
All rights reserved Judith Auslander, M.A., PCC
ISBN is 1478239506 and ISBN-13 is 987-1478239505

What Others Are Saying About
The Power Of Goal Setting

Awesome book! The words flow as if you were hearing from a friend -- and you are! Well worth reading.

Kim Blanquie, Summit Leadership Coaching

The Power of Goal Setting is so easy to follow! The writing is simple, yet precise and clear. I can tell that Judith has specific goals she wants to convey to the readers. I like the fact that she uses so many examples that area easy to relate to, and she has a great sense of humor! It's fun reading! If a reader follows her directions and suggestions, she or he will gain a lot out of this"

Yumiko Freeman, Student of Oriental Medicine and Acupuncture

This positive and non-intimidating manual is easy to use. It provides the reader exercises and charts to analyze issues. Suggestions, tools and checklists help initiate change turning dreams into goals and achievements. I'm glad to have it!

Jennifer Bush

As she states at the beginning of the workbook, there is nothing new in its contents. What is new and what is effective are two different matters. Judith Auslander's *The Power of Goal Setting* is effective. She has created something like a warm, comforting hand to hold, and a pair of light weight, cushioned, yet supportive, shoes to wear while she walks with you through the process of goal setting. This enables the reader to accomplish the second part - *Transforming Thoughts Into Action* - in a manner that is quick, satisfying and has lasting benefits.
I read the entire workbook and completed all the exercises in four days of only bedtime reading, but I continue to receive daily benefits from the process. And it is comforting to know that Judith Auslander is at the other end of electronic mail or telephone line when I need coaching and encouragement in meeting my goals.

Beverlee Patton-Allen

Dedication

Most every book has a dedication. Why? Because, as John Donne (1572-1631), stated, "No man (or woman in this case) is an island." I am not an island. There are many people who have supported me through this endeavor whom I wish to thank. I know that I will miss some of you, and in advance I say, thank you. You know who you are, and I stand taller because I stood on your shoulders.

The first person I want to thank is my sister (Fribling) Debbie. She and I walk very different paths in life. I know that she doesn't always understand my path – but she is always there beside me. As she puts it, "I have your back sis." I am not always sure what having my back means, but I do know that her love and support is always and continuously there. For us, older and younger sibling is long past – we are simply there for each other.

So, I knew when it came to this workbook that I could go to Debbie and ask her if she would help me by editing it. She has much greater skills in this area than I do (in fact, she will probably critique this entire dedication). She has taken hours of her time on the phone with me to go over every single line of this book. I mean – every single word, dash, comma, question mark and exclamation point. We would argue about how a sentence structure would sound better. And we laughed – OMG – how we laughed. Sometimes, I will use a word that may sound something like what I am trying to say, but has an entirely different meaning. I know that all I have to do is mention the word "dollop" now and we will have a good laugh. I know that our Dad is looking down on us from heaven, watching us working together, and "kvelling*." Thank you Fribling!

I want to thank all my clients as they have helped me as much as I have helped them. Coaching is not done in isolation – it is a give and take of energy – so I have received much from my clients – and I thank them.

I must, and dearly want, to thank all my wonderful supportive friends. There are so many of you – The Wild Hatties, my Bahá'í sisters, and all the sisters and brothers and my "adopted" children I have gathered along the way. You have supported and loved me and it is because of that love and support that I was able to write this book. You believed in me so that I was able to believe in myself.

I dedicate this book to all of you,

Judith Auslander, 2008 Revised in 2012
* Kvelling – Yiddish word – "To beam with pride and pleasure."

Disclaimer

I stand by everything that is written in this book. If you disagree with any part, please feel free to contact me about it.

Since I am sure some of you are wondering where the "Parts" all being about coffee came from. The truth is, I cannot actually say how it happened. It started with a sentence and ended up continuing throughout the book. No, I am not a coffee addict, but I do enjoy a good cup of coffee or chai or tea.

Thank you for purchasing this book. I hope that you will find it inspiring and useful. I would love to hear of your successes or even where you might be hung up. Please feel free to contact me by going to my website www.WiseHeartCoaching.com and fill in the form. I promise I will write or call you back.

WORKSHOPS:

I am also available to do a workshop on this book. If you are interested in my coming to your area to put on a 6-8 hour workshop either in one day or a series of 3 to 4 sessions, please just send me a note from my website www.WiseHeartCoaching.com and fill in the form. I promise that everyone will not only learn about goal setting, but also have a lot of fun at the same time.

Table of Contents

Page 1	Introduction
Page 2	Part I – A goal for a good cup of coffee is a dream your heart makes. (Taking your dreams off Someday Island and onto the Road to Success)
Page 2	Part II – Success is drinking a good cup of coffee and not spilling a drop on your shirt. (What is success?)
Page 4	Part III – I fear if I drink any more coffee I will not sleep tonight. (Fear of failure.)
Page 6	Part IV - Would you like that goal with cream or sugar? (What is a goal?)
Page 9	Part V – Do I want a squirt of almond flavoring in my coffee? (How values and goals work together.)
Page 11	Part VI – Could you please tell me about all your different kinds of lattes? (What kind of goal to set?)
Page 13	Part VII – Too many choices, too many questions, coffee, latte, tea, chai? (Questions to ask about your goals.)
Page 15	Part VIII – Let me see I was to get 3 lattes – 1 skinny, 1 with a shot of … oh, what was it????? (The first step to setting a goal.)
Page 16	Part IX – Which SMART steps do I follow to the local coffee joint? (S.M.A.R.T. rules)
Page 18	Part X – Do I want a Short, Tall, Grande or Venti – what does Venti mean? (Baby steps.)
Page 20	Part XI - I thought we wanted a Chai Tea – how did we end up with a latte? (Self-Sabotage!)
Page 22	Part XII – One, two, three lumps of sugar and dollop of cream please. (Get organized!)
Page 24	Part XIII – As long as I have some extra time – I think I will stop here and enjoy a cup of tea. Oh, and maybe read a magazine, call a friend… (Time wasters.)

Page 27	Part XIV - Did you say you wanted a cup of coffee or an exotic latte with that goal? (Stinkin' Thinkin' and Affirmations.)
Page 32	Part XV – Ah, let me write a sonnet of my love for the java bean let me count the beans? Number One … (Journaling)
Page 34	Part XVI – I not only woke up and smelled the coffee – I actually see the coffee. (Visualization.)
Page 37	Part XVII – Do you have a copy of Coffee Lovers Magazine? (Reading)
Page 38	Part XVIII – I can see it all now – life without coffee is impossible. (Vision Board.)
Page 40	Part XIX – Tea is much more fun with two for tea. (Support Team.)
Page 44	Part XX – I drank all the coffee I need and it is time to say adieu – to you and you and you. (After the goal is completed.)
Page 45	Part XXI – Next on the list – a good chocolate store – or maybe coffee mocha ice cream! (Celebration!)
Page 46	Part XXII – May I have a little "OMMMM" with my Chai? (Our higher self.)
Page 49	Sources
Page 52	Worksheets information

Worksheets Table of Contents in the Worksheet Section

"I just closed the deal on my first full kitchen order, only 7 more to go this year! Business is booming!" Julie Capps (Workshop Participant)

"I did get all my debts to friends paid off. I was giving myself until Dec. 31 of this year but got it done last Thursday night." Jane McIver (Workshop Participant)

INTRODUCTION

> `Cheshire Puss,' she began, rather timidly, as she did not at all know whether it would like the name: however, it only grinned a little wider. `Come, it's pleased so far,' thought Alice, and she went on. `Would you tell me, please, which way I ought to go from here?'
> 'That depends a good deal on where you want to get to,' said the Cat.
> `I don't much care where--' said Alice.
> `Then it doesn't matter which way you go,' said the Cat.
> `--so long as I get somewhere,' Alice added as an explanation.
> `Oh, you're sure to do that,' said the Cat, `if you only walk long enough.'
> – Lewis Carroll from Alice's Adventures in Wonderland

Have you ever boarded a bus without any idea of where you are going? Just got on the bus and said to the driver – onward? Have you ever taken an exam without the slightest idea of what answers to write or even what subject it was? Or have you ever lifted the phone without any idea of whom to call and talk to – just dialed a number? Probably not!

The thing is that when you board the bus you have a goal of somewhere that you desire to go. When you take your exam you know (or hopefully know) what the subject is and the responses to the questions and your goal is to probably pass the test. When you lift the phone to make a call you have a goal of the person you want to talk to and why. We set goals all the time – we just may not think about it as a goal.

Goal setting is required so you will be able to reap the valuable fruits of your efforts. The strategy of goal setting is needed in attaining what you truly desire. Goal setting serves as an outline of the plans you engage yourself in and include the reason as to why you need to obtain them. Goals must be definite and they must be achievable. The challenge is how to make goal-setting fun, easy and successful.

Part I – A goal for a good cup of coffee is a dream your heart makes.

A dream becomes a goal when action is taken toward its achievement.
– Bo Bennett

Most goals start as dreams. The thing is most dreams just remain that – a dream. A dream and a goal are very different. A dream is a wish, a hope, or a desire. The problem is that most people do not know how to take a dream and change it into a goal. So, there lay your dreams basking in the sun on Someday Island, while you slave away in the Land of Reality. The question is how do you get your dreams off of Someday Island and get them on the Road To Reality and Success? Well, there are many, many methods, and I am going to teach a few of them to you. I have to tell you though, I like to have fun with my goals, so I will include lots of ways to have fun and enjoy the process.

So, let's start by getting those dreams off the island and on the road to success. Ready?

It takes as much energy to wish as it does to plan
– Eleanor Roosevelt

Part II – Success is drinking a good cup of coffee and not spilling a drop on your shirt.

"Eighty percent of success is showing up."
– Woody Allen

There are thousands of quotes on success, but one of the best that I have ever read was, "Success is the completion of anything intended" (author unknown). The author went on to say that robbing a bank could be viewed as a success if that is what you intended. However, poor planning probably is what sent him/her to jail.

The basic concept is to create a plan, make it a goal, and follow it through to its completion. Easy!! If you don't make a plan or do not follow your plan (or you end up in jail) your goal will more than likely have failed.

What is success to you? This is a very important question. According to best selling author Brian Tracy, "Success is goals, and all else is commentary." He believes that people with clear, written goals, accomplish far more in a shorter period of time than people without them.

Discipline is a major factor in success. Just saying you are going to do something does not get it done. You must be disciplined in your carrying out the steps toward your goal in order to achieve success and what that means to you.

A good example is the person who says they want to write a book. Stating you want to write a book does not get it done. However, stating you are going to write a book and you are committed to write for one hour every day, that is a goal. By the time a year has passed, and if the commitment has been met, the writer will have written 365 hours. Think about it! This person will more than likely have success in their goal and have written a book.

So, the question begs to be asked. If you plan something and it doesn't work out the way it was intended – or it fails – is "failure" actually failure? You must decide this for yourself, but for me failure is a learning experience. (I will write more in Part III.)
Failure is just the other side of the coin of success. Just because it is heads instead of tails, is the coin worth anything less? No, both have equal earning power. It is just that if you said "tails" and it came up "heads" you lose the bet – you are still the same person.

> Success is the ability to go from one failure to another with no loss of enthusiasm.
> – Sir Winston Churchill

Part III – I fear if I drink any more coffee I will not sleep tonight.

> *Life is like riding a bicycle. You don't fall off unless you stop pedaling.*
> – Claude Pepper

Why do so many people start goals only to fail? Mostly because of fear! What? How can people fear a goal? Well, actually it is not the goal they fear but rather fear of FAILURE and fear of SUCCESS, and most people have both.

Fear of failure is pretty understandable. You know what failure feels like – we have all failed at something in our lifetime. The thing about it is how we deal with that failure. Some people just stuff new failures into their satchel of failures and drag the whole mess along with them right onto the next one. I once knew a woman who, based on her life long list of failures, named herself Princess Shit Walker. Really!

Oh, and by the way, that woman was me!

Failure became a part of my life. So much so that I started to expect it – and worse of all – accept it and not learn from it. We all fail at something – it is just that I choose to no longer call it failure – instead I call it a "learning experience." If I make a mistake I say, "OK, learning experience and I won't do that one again." I decided to learn.

> *The greatest barrier to success is the fear of failure.*
> – Sven Goran Eriksson
>
> *In order to succeed, your desire for success should be greater than your fear of failure*
> – Bill Cosby

The other fear is the fear of success. Fear of success?? Yes, we fear success. What happens once I succeed? What will people expect of me if I succeed? Will I be expected to always succeed? Can I fail once I succeed? We seem to judge people even more if they succeeded and then have a failure. So much so that it becomes almost too difficult to succeed.

Also, there is the problem with dealing with success. Success can change everything. If we succeed will our family and friends treat us differently? Will I be allowed to just be me – will more be expected of me? Will I be able to deliver? We have so many fears around success that some have actually chosen failure over success. Look at what has happened to the people who have won the lottery. Most lottery winners, according to research, lose their money within 5 years after the win. I believe it is due to fear of success. We don't know how to handle it. We are not trained to handle success. Failure is something that we are actually more trained to handle than success. Think about how you would react if when you walked into a room, people stood up and they applauded you. Could you handle that much positive attention? It might sound good, but just thinking about it how hot are your cheeks getting? How much has your blood pressure gone up? Wouldn't you rather just go back behind that curtain and hide? Probably a lot! We are not trained for success. We are conditioned for failure.

There is a lot more to write about fear and goals and I work with clients on these issues. However, for this book on goal setting, this is enough. I suggest that if you know you have fears (and who doesn't) that you work with a trained coach to change your fears into freedom.

Part IV - Would you like that goal with cream or sugar?

Have you tired to reach a goal that seems unattainable? Do you often decide that you will do something that will change your life like lose weight, save money, exercise more, keep the house clean, read instead of watch TV, learn to knit ... and then time passes and nothing happens – nothing changes? Maybe you start out with great intentions, but your goal still sits there waiting for you.

Well, you are not alone. I have searched for statistics on this very human behavior, but could not find any exact measurement. What I did discover is that most goals are NOT achieved because people do NOT do the necessary work.

When you were a child, were you lucky enough to have grown-ups that practiced goal setting? Did the family sit down together and plan how all of you would work together to afford a trip to Disneyland? Each family member provided with a way that they would support the team effort to afford this holiday? If you had these kinds of grown-ups around you as a child, you are very lucky and you probably learned some wonderful goal setting tools.

If you are like most people and did not grow up with goal setting in your family, then this book will teach you how to set and achieve goals.

My goal is to help you achieve your goals by making the work simple, easy, clear, measurable and persuasive enough so you will follow through. That is my goal. What is yours?

There are hundreds of articles, books and speakers telling you how to set goals. There are methods beyond measurement. Yet, I believe in the tried and true method, which is

SMART (see Part IX). I believe the first step is having a desire for the goal surrounded by your passion in achieving it.

> Touch passion when it comes your way…It's rare enough as it is. Don't walk away when it calls you by name.
> – J. Michael Straczynski

So the question begs to be asked, how much of goal setting and achieving really relies on passion? Well, actually a lot. If there is no passion behind your goal – it more than likely will not happen. If your goal is to write a book but you really have no vision of that book, no real desire to write, I don't care if you follow every step I will outline for you – you more than likely will not write that book. And if you do write it, there will be little feeling of joy in its completion.

The same goes for wanting to lose weight. If your doctor, family, friends, the mirror tells you to lose weight, but you don't really want to lose weight or are happy the way you are – you will not lose weight. Why? Because there is no passion, you are not using words and thoughts that are going to motivate you to follow through. Somehow, someway you will cheat (only yourself) and stop the diet and eat that ice cream sundae because you deserve it. You will skip that workout because you don't feel like it. You will sabotage yourself because it is not really what you want. You may think you want it, but in reality you are happy the way you are.

The key is, you must have some feeling, some passion, some real reason for wanting to achieve that goal.

What is really interesting is that this passion for a goal has nothing to do with age. I had the bounty of having a 14-year-old girl (let's call her Tina) in one of my goal setting classes. Tina came with her parents. I wasn't sure how this would work, but went ahead and added her to the class roster. Tina became one of the stars of the class. Her goal was to purchase a guitar and lessons. She deeply and passionately wanted to play the guitar. Prior to the class Tina had been begging her parents for a guitar. Like most teens she felt that her parents "should" buy it for her. During the class she became motivated to pay for the guitar and lessons herself. Through planning her goals out, she set steps toward purchasing her own guitar and lessons.

About 2 months after the class ended I received a phone call from Tina. She called to let me know that she had achieved her goal. She had just purchased an acoustical guitar and was learning chords as we spoke. The pride and thrill in her voice was crystal clear. Hers was a successful goal!

Kids get it! Kids really get goal setting. The best part of kids learning about goals is that it teaches them some real values. In this "get it now," "I want it now," immediate gratification world, kids learn the value of patience and real earned pride.

I believe that goal setting is something that kids could be easily taught in school – starting in grade school. We have a real problem when kids are told what to do, when to do it, never set their own goals. What happens is that they graduate from high school and say, "Now what?" They go on to college where again they are told what to do and when to do it. Without being taught how to set real life goals, once again they leave school, university in this case, and say, "Now what?" Wouldn't school be more fun, be filled with more passion, if goal setting were a part of it? I think so.

> The more intensely we feel about an idea or a goal, the more assuredly the idea, buried deep in our subconscious, will direct us along the path to its fulfillment.
> – Earl Nightingale

Part V – Do I want a squirt of almond flavoring in my coffee?

> We're so engaged in doing things to achieve purposes of outer value that we forget that the inner value, the rapture that is associated with being alive, is what it's all about.
> – Joseph Campbell

One question that must be asked does the goal match my values? If your goal is not a part of your values you will have a very difficult time achieving it. This is extremely important. We may have dreams on Someday Island, but that is where they are meant to stay. They are meant to be just that – a dream. Why? Usually, because they are either not really a passion or they do not fit our values.

As a coach, the first assignment I give all my clients is the values test – you will find this included in the workbook. Until you know your values, you will be fighting an uphill battle toward your goals. Let's say you want to earn a 6-figure income. You decide you want to get a job working for a company where you will be making a successful income (according to your values) and be seen by the world as a success. This sounds great – but it would be best to make sure that job is one that meets squarely with your values. If you do not, than you may attain that job, you may earn that really great income, but you may also be quite miserable. In her book, *Finding Your Own North Star,* Martha Beck talks about how it is important to know your "essential self" and your "social self," and which one is in control of the work you choose. Your essential self has been there since you were born, but your social self has been overtaking your essential self since you began to take a part in the world around you. Your social self may be the one leading you toward that 6-figure income while your essential self is miserable.

From *Blueprinting – Living Your Life By Design and Not Chance* – "Happiness - Far too many people in our society go through life without zest and enthusiasm. Frequently this is because they are doing things and being things that are not congruent with who they are. The result can be burnout, depression and ineffectiveness. The key is to check what is important to you and then make sure your life is in synch with that."

Dr. Phil McGraw is an excellent example. In his book, *Self Matters,* he starts the book with a young man standing in a parking lot calling his father to tell him the really great news that he had graduated as a doctor. For eleven years this young man went to school to become a doctor. His family wanted him to become a doctor (his father was one) so it was expected that he would become a doctor. Here is this young man ready to call his Dad with what should have been a glorious moment suddenly turning into the realization that he had no desire to be a doctor. He had followed the path that he was "suppose" to follow – not the one that was a part of his true values. It took Dr. Phil eleven years to realize this. Some people find out sooner, but most live their entire adult life never realizing that they are not happy because they are not living their values.

Another way we see goals that are misaligned is if your goal is to earn a lot of money. Let's say you have a business and you want to see the money rolling in proving that the business is successful. However, when you take your values test you find that "money" does not come up as one of your top 5 values – in fact, it comes in as one of the bottom 5. I find this happens with many clients. So, how can you want to earn a lot of money when money is not part of your value system? In fact, you probably have some real issues around money. You will want to do some work on money issues and the blocks around it. And boy, do we have blocks around money!!

Before you set a goal free from Someday Island, make sure that it fits your values. If it doesn't fit, and it is something you really desire, then you will want to do some work on changing your feelings and emotions around that value. To change a value from your bottom 5 to your top 5 will take a lot of work – but it can be done. I will discuss a couple of ways to create this change. One way is to hire a professional coach. That is what coaching does; it helps you regain control of your life so that you can live the life you deserve.

> It's not hard to make decisions when you know what your values are.
> – Roy Disney (Nephew of Walt Disney)

Part VI – Could you please tell me about all your different kinds of lattes?

> You have brains in your head,
> you have feet in your shoes
> you can steer yourself
> in any direction you choose.
> – Theodor Seuss Geisel (Dr. Seuss)

Maybe you are unsure of what your goal should be. Maybe you have too many ideas and no idea which one to pursue first. Or maybe you are just at a loss of where to start. Here are some ideas for where to look in your life where goals might fit.

- **Art, Drama, Writing:** Look at where you may want to develop in these areas. Is there a dream of putting the arts into your life?
- **Career:** Have you been thinking about changing your career or job, or maybe going to school so you might advance in your career.

- **Family:** Perhaps you have been thinking about getting married or making the relationship you have a deeper, better one. Or possibly you have been wanting to plan a huge family get together or event. You may be considering adding to your family by having or adopting children. Maybe you have been thinking how you can mend a relationship with a parent, child or other family member. If marriage or better relationship or having children is a goal, perhaps taking classes to be a better partner or parent might be a goal.
- **Financial:** How much do you want to earn? Is investment in a business a goal? Maybe your goal is start saving more and spending less.
- **Volunteering:** Perhaps you have been thinking about giving back to your community through volunteering. You will need to talk to your significant others and find out how it will affect their lives. You will want to investigate various places and evaluate if their needs meet your needs.
- **Physical:** Do you feel it is time to put more effort into being physically fit? This might mean investigating gyms and health clubs. If your goal is to eat better, consider taking a nutrition class.
- **Pleasure and Fun:** Are you looking to add more fun and pleasure to your life? Are the scales balanced between your work and social life?
- **Attitude:** Do you want to change your attitude – be more positive and hopeful? Will your success increase if you change your relationship attitude with money or other parts of your life that might be getting in the way?
- **Travel:** Maybe you want to see more of your country or maybe the world. Do you want to go for a week, two weeks, a month, 6 months, a year? Do you want it to be a part of your business or work or do you

want it to be totally pleasure? Do you want to see what it is like to live in another country? I did, and spent 4 ½ years living and working in El Salvador. Many goals can be written around travel.

I was in the drug store the other day trying to get a cold medication... Not easy. There's an entire wall of products you need. You stand there going, Well, this one is quick acting but this is long lasting... Which is more important, the present or the future?
– Jerry Seinfeld

Part VII – Too many choices, too many questions, coffee, latte, tea, chai?

Goals cannot be set without thinking about a number of other very important aspects. First of all you cannot just say, "I want this or I want that." Generally, people will say things like, "I want to lose weight" or "I want a new job" or "I want to get married." The problem is that is all the effort they put into it. Without direction, these are just words. In order to have successful goal consider the following questions.

- **Is there anything you must do first before you can achieve your goal?** Do you need additional education, take a specialized class, or pass a certification exam? Make sure you have all your ducks (or degrees) in a row ready for when you go for your goal. I have a friend who wants to own his own construction business. He must first pass the state exam in order to get his license, attain the necessary insurance, purchase all necessary tools, hire employees – this is all before he can hang his shingle as a construction business owner.
- **Who is going to be involved in this goal?** Since you probably do not operate in a complete and total vacuum, someone else is going to be affected by this goal. Let's look at me for a second – I am not married, my son is a grown man, I have little family left. So, one might think

that a goal I make would not really affect anyone other than myself. But this is not true. When I am working on a goal I have my support team involved (more on support teams later.) I may not be able to spend as much time with friends as I am busy working on my goal. My conversation may be tilted toward talking about my goal. I may be more focused on what I am heading for than other things. It is important to think of who will be involved and affected by your goal. You want to make sure that everyone is behind you pushing in the same direction. You do not want anyone out there who might sabotage you.

- The next important question is: **What do you exactly want to accomplish?** If you are not clear – then your goal is going to be just as unclear. Having a goal to lose weight does not really mean anything. One-pound loss is losing weight. You must be very clear about exactly what your goal is. Instead of, "I want to lose weight," state, "I want to lose 25 pounds by a specific date." The same goes if you want to get married (which by the way is several goals), then you need to state exactly the kind of person you want to marry and by when. Your goal will be as abstract as you are unclear.

- **Where will your goal be accomplished?** Will it be in the town you are presently living in or will it be somewhere else. There is an old saying, "If you don't know where you're going, any road will take you there." People of great achievement know exactly where they are going and they take the necessary steps to get there. But you have to decide where "there" is for you.

- **When will you accomplish this goal?** Again, the date is part of clarity. It must be clear and concise. It also cannot be too close so that you feel too much pressure or too far away that you get loosy goosy about when it will happen. It also is a great way to end up sabotaging yourself.

- **Why do you want to achieve this goal?** It is important to really know your reason for going after your goal. If you are unsure it is going to make it very difficult to stay on track and to not self-sabotage (more on this later.)

The best way to answer the above questions is to sit down with a blank sheet of paper and respond to each one with thought and care. It will not do you any good to go head long into goal setting without addressing these very important issues first.

Part VIII – Let me see I was to get 3 lattes – 1 skinny, 1 with a shot of... oh, what was it??????

> All that we are is the result of what we have thought. The mind is everything. What we think, we become.
> – Buddha

Write your goals down on paper. There are hundreds people walking around with goals stuck in their heads, but have never been written on paper. Here is the thing about that. It doesn't work. If your goal is not written down, it won't get done – unless you happen to be the most disciplined person in the world. If you are like most people, you will need to write down your goals. Why does writing work where just leaving it in your head will not? It is because the act of writing it down starts it down the path of reality. While it is in your head it has no time line, no real guides, nothing about it is real. It is merely thoughts.

As you write down your goal and all its attributes it takes on more energy becoming more real. It becomes a living, breathing entity. The more detail, the more alive it becomes, the more alive it becomes, the more chance it has of success. As it is with this book that you are reading, it started with an idea. It then bloomed into an outline, which became a class. It then took on even more life force as it flowered into this manuscript. This book didn't happen just because I thought, "Oh someday I want to write a book." I did think that for a long time. However, it did not manifest until I wrote it down. Writing has power. Yes, thoughts have power, but until you put it on paper, it does not fully become alive.

Of course the last step is to take action. And the rest of the book will tell you how to do that.

> The pen is the tongue of the mind.
> – Miguel de Cervantes

Part IX – Which SMART steps do I follow to the local coffee joint?

> I have discovered in life that there are ways of getting almost anywhere you want to go, if you really want to go.
> – Langston Hughes

Goal setting is a skill - a skill learned like any other, such as playing the piano, balancing a checkbook, or how to study. It's not something that a few lucky people were born with. Therefore, it comes with tools that will aid you in improving your skills. In goal setting, that skill is spelled SMART(S).

S   Specific:

You've probably all heard how important it is to have a very specific goal. Do you know why? A specific goal has a much better chance of being accomplished than a vague/general goal. Frustration and confusion can be created when it's difficult to tell whether you're really on the right track. Instead you know you're headed toward something specific, like Seattle, instead of just "north".

M   Motivational/Meaningful:

In order to succeed with a goal, it has to have a certain emotional power to excite you enough to let you be willing to spend the time and effort necessary to achieve it. Are you excited by your goal? What's your motive? What's your motivation? How can you make it meaningful to you? Do you really want it?

A   Acceptable:

Is this something that you want for yourself? Do you accept this goal and the effort and time it will require of you? Are you willing and able to work towards this goal? A goal is acceptable to you when you feel comfortable with it, and believe that you can accomplish it. If you don't believe in it, it will not believe in you.

R   Realistic/Real to Me:

Is the goal realistic for you? Is it real to you? Can you see yourself in the future when the goal is reached? What do you look like, what are you doing, where are you doing it? What does it smell like, feel like, taste like? Get all your body senses involved. Your goal has to be something you can visualize yourself doing. If you can't imagine it, you won't do it.

T   Trackable/Target Date:

A goal must have a target date to be motivating and to help you focus. A deadline too far in the future is subject to "Someday Island." A goal that's too tight, too confining is discouraging. Set your target date based on small milestones; like how many classes you need to take for training, or losing 1 pound per week. Avoid setting yourself up for frustration and therefore setting yourself up to fail.

S   Selebration:

OK, this is one that I am adding. It is Selebration (Celebration). It is best to include some sort of reward for following through and achieving your goal. Have a list of different rewards that you can give yourself. Rewards are very motivating and can keep you on track and keep you from self-sabotaging.

> I am here for a purpose and that purpose is to grow into a mountain, not to shrink to a grain of sand. Henceforth will I apply ALL my efforts to become the highest mountain of all and I will strain my potential until it cries for mercy.
> – Og Mandino

Part X – Do I want a Short, Tall, Grande or Venti – what does Venti mean?

> When it is obvious that the goals cannot be reached, don't adjust the goals, adjust the action steps
> – Confucius

It is time to start putting it all together. The first step is to write down your goal clearly and distinctly. For example: My goal is to open a donut shop.

Now, the second step is to Think Small. What, you may be asking is she thinking? Isn't she supposed to be a life coach and thinking big? Why would I want to think small? Well, my response to this is – what's wrong with small? Remember, good things come in small packages. And in this case, small means lots and lots of time for celebrating – and you already know I like to celebrate.

What I am talking about is taking small baby steps in your goals. One of my favorite ways of doing this is through first doing Reverse Planning (explained in the worksheet section). After you have completed reverse planning, then take these steps and break them down into baby steps. Each step completed is a time to celebrate.

Let's say as part of your donut shop you want to build a website. Building a website is a HUGE step – definitely not a baby step. It might be one of the steps on your reverse planning sheet, but it is an entire goal in and of itself. Building a website has a number of baby steps in it such as:

1. Investigate different website builders and templates.
2. Design the type of website I want.
3. Work on ideas for page one of my website
4. Start working on page one

You will want to take all the steps from the reverse planning and create a goal development sheet (in the worksheet section) for each one of these.

It is important to not always think big – big can be scary and lead to self-sabotage or burnout. You want many successes to keep you motivated and on track. Remember when you were a kid and your mom put those wonderful colored stars on a chart that would eventually lead to something special? Just to let you know, we never outgrew that need for star charts.

Part XI - I thought we wanted a Chai Tea – how did we end up with a latte?

> Our subconscious mind can be compared to a garden - if we leave it unattended, the weeds will grow wild. Goal setting quotes are a great destroyer of those weeds.
> – Dr. Joseph Murphy

So, what is going on here? You are going along doing everything to achieve your goal when suddenly you find that you are self-sabotaging? What's the deal here? Here is the bad news, we all self-sabotage in some way. If you don't know that you self-sabotage, then you are living on the river called Denial. The key is to understand why.

I have mentioned the absolute need to have passion around your goal. So, you know if there is no passion you will probably not succeed in your goal. I have also written the necessity for the goal to match our values. You already know that if the goals and values don't match, you will generally self-sabotage.

Now, here is the good news, you are not alone. That's right! There are many, many different parts of you that live inside your brain. No, you are not schizophrenic. It is just different parts of you that have been created over your life span. These different parts have their role and purpose, but often what they do is distract and sabotage you. They are not evil or mean spirited; they simply have a different agenda. The question is how do you get these different parts on your team? Well, you have to talk to them and get them on board. There is a method to achieving this.

First of all you need to remember to treat each part with respect. It is a part of you – remember that. So, let's say you are dealing with the part of you that believes that every time something bad happens to you or you feel bad that you must eat chocolate, chips or some kind of junk food in order to feel better. The problem is – you want to lose weight. You are on this new eating regime that completely eliminates the food the part inside you wants in order to feel good. What to do? You are going to talk to it – and the best way to do this is through journaling.

Start by first calling that part of you that is sabotaging you forward and ask it if it will converse with you. You can give it a name, even a particular character development – have fun with it. Thank it for its time. Thank this part of you for wanting to take care of you by helping you feel better by eating junk or sugary food. It has been a friend and a caretaker. To be angry or mean to this part of yourself is not going to do either of you any good. You must be loving, thoughtful and thankful. However, you will want to explain how this food is not really doing you any good and you would like to stop eating it. You will ask this part of yourself what you may replace the junk food with. Once an agreement is made then thank this part of you. You may even give it a new job, title, something to make it feel welcome and necessary. Remember, this is a part of you and needs to be respected and loved. This whole thing may sound childish and almost simpleton, but I challenge you to work on something you want to change by not engaging in some kind of dialogue with yourself. Dialoguing with your different parts is a necessity.

According to Portland, Oregon author, Alyce Cornyn-Selby who wrote *What's Your Sabotage*, there are many different "Directors" inside of you. She named several different Directors including the Financial, Social, Time Keeper, and the Inner Child. I have also discovered the Inner Critic, the Know it All, The Fearful Child and The Snob. You must talk to all involved. Sometimes you may think it is the Inner Child that is sabotaging your goal to stay organized, but it may just be your Social Director who does not want to invest the time in cleaning the desk and would rather be out dancing – and you are not listening to him/her. Instead you want to work and it wants to play. There might even be others involved in sabotaging your clean desk, so it is best to look inside and invite them all forward for a round table discussion. If not, the self-sabotage will continue. Think of them as the Board of Directors. If you had a meeting and did not email all the board members and let them know about it – well you can just imagine the results.

What this is basically doing is helping you to know who is in charge of making the decisions you make without fully knowing why. I am sure this has happened to you where you do something and wondered why in the heck you did that. This is what happens when we are not communicating with all our various parts, their needs, and their desires. You need to know what makes you tick. You will know yourself a lot better. If you are to set goals, you want all the board members working as a team. Otherwise, it will be an uphill battle.

> The point of knowing your internal parts is just that: knowing them. By knowing them, you know yourself.
> – Cobar Pita

Part XII – One, two, three lumps of sugar and dollop of cream please.

So, you want to set and achieve a goal – well – GET ORGANIZED!!

Oh, I am sorry; did I hit a sore point?

Well, in order to have success with your goal setting you are going to need to get organized. Clean up the desk, organize your files, clean out the in-basket and by all means, clean up the "to do" list. I have included a wonderful sheet called the "Tah Dah" list, which was created by a friend of mine – you will find it in the worksheet section. Make photocopies of it and use it. Get those small chores that just seem to lie around waiting to get done – done. Hummm!!! Things like one I have sitting here in front of me right now as I type. I have a small desk lamp that seems to have blown its light bulb. Now all I have to do is check to make sure it is plugged in and if that is not the problem, change the bulb if it is the problem. It is small things like my lamp, which can weigh on your mind and keep from the real task – getting those goals accomplished.

The other thing to get organized is your time. Without time management there is a lot of wasted time. I am a big believer that the first goal in goal setting is to make a list of things to get done each day. Be realistic – setting too many in a day can only bring disappointment or self-sabotage. I even go so far as to list how long a chore might take. I list everything I plan to accomplish in a day – even the small – taken for granted tasks. Why? Because the best part of having a list is crossing things off. As I complete a task I scratch it off. The list also keeps me on target – what I planned to do and what I get done. I even put them in order of priority so that way, what needs to get done first, gets done. What tasks do not get completed go on the next day's list. Checklists work!

> It's kind of fun to do the impossible
> – Walt Disney

**...s I have some extra time – I think I will stop here and
. Oh, and maybe read a magazine, call a friend…**

t it's priceless. You can't own it, but you can use it. You can't keep it but
it. Once you've lost it you can never get it back.
Kay

We all waste time. It is natural. How much of your time wasting actually self-sabotages you in achieving your goal? If you find that the day has gone by and you have not accomplished what was on your "to do" list, then perhaps you are a time waster.

Often we waste time due to fear. When you may be fearful of what an outcome may be – such as fear of going out and marketing your business – you become amazingly resourceful at finding things to occupy your time.

Have you ever watched a child that has been sent to their room to clean it? They suddenly become entranced by something and an hour later nothing in the room has budged. When you ask the child what she/he has been doing – she/he will probably say, "I don't know." How many adults do exactly the same thing? You may have a resume' to work on, or a letter to write – and the day goes by and it isn't done. It isn't that you haven't been doing something. You could probably list a number of chores you accomplished in the day. However, none of those chores led to getting what you really wanted to get done – done.

Here is a list of some time wasters. See if any of them fit you.
- Turning on the TV and suddenly becoming engrossed in a program – an hour goes by.
- Turning on the computer to just check your email – hours go by (this is my biggest time waster.)
- Calling a friend to chat for only a few minutes…..right!

- Deciding to relax at the computer and play a few games or search the Internet for an item.
- You are really focused on what you are doing and the telephone rings or a visitor stops by.

This is only a small list of the numerous things that sabotage our daily list of things to get done. Let's see what you can do about some of these time wasters.

- If the telephone is a constant interrupter – set it to silent and decide a time to go and pick up your messages. You do not have to be a slave to the phone ringing.
- If emails are your disruption, then make a plan to not open your email until you have accomplished what you have set out to do. This will mean not even opening your email up. This will avoid that pleasant little "chime" or pop-up whenever an email has come in. Even if email is important for your business, put looking at it on your "to do" list. I guarantee that you will get more done if you are not constantly going back and forth between emails and your work. I coached a young man who was feeling frustrated with his banking work because he did not have time for everything he wanted to get done in a day. I asked him about his email usage and discovered that the minute he came into the office he would turn on his email. Checking over his email would end up occupying a great part of his morning. We decided that instead of checking his email first thing in the morning, he make a list of what he wanted to get done, prioritize it, and stay focused on that. On the list was checking his email, and when that item came up, he would check it

then. Since he has done this, he accomplishes much more and feeling he has more control of his day.

- Do not turn on the TV. If you really cannot stand it – hide the remote or the batteries.
- If the computer is not part of your work – do not turn it on. Put a piece of tape over the power button.

You can discover all kinds of fun ways to avoid time wasters. Remember, it is always a choice. If you find you are unable to stop yourself, hiring a coach would help. I am not suggesting that you don't take time in your day to relax. Relaxing and taking a break is anything but a time waster. Taking time for you is important. In fact, you will probably have more energy afterward than if you had not taken a break. The point is to not take too many breaks or spend several hours on a break. This will mean timing your breaks. If you know that you are a time waster, then it would probably help to monitor yourself a little more closely. You can do this with a timer, asking a friend to call you in 30 minutes to remind you to get back on task, you could even have your mother call you! Let's hope it doesn't go that far.

Another form of time wasting is procrastination. Procrastination is often the death of dreams. We procrastinate so long that deadlines pass, time expires, jobs and opportunities are lost. More money is lost due to procrastination. So, what can you do about this thief?

Lists will help – but only if you follow through. Hiring a coach will help you discover why you procrastinate and how to eliminate it. I suggest that you journal with the part of you that holds to the false belief that procrastinating is "just what I do." Procrastination is a choice. I could say, "Make a different choice," but I realize it is not that simple.

Procrastination is almost like a disease that needs to be rooted out, operated on, removed. If procrastination is running your life, I suggest you do something about it – and soon.

> We say we waste time, but that is impossible. We waste ourselves.
> – Alice Bolch

Part XIV - Did you say you wanted a cup of coffee or an exotic latte with that goal?

> To come to be you must have a vision of Being, a Dream, a Purpose, a Principle. You will become what your vision is.
> – Peter Nivio Zarlenga

First, how you state your goals is extremely important. Do you say, "I hate my job and must find a new one or I will go crazy?" What happens if you say instead, "I am looking forward to the opportunity of looking for a new job that will be more stimulating and rewarding?" Which one is more motivating? Which one sounds more positive? The problem is that when you think or say negative words, you actually are creating exactly what you are thinking. You see, there is this part of you called the subconscious and it is wonderful part of you – it is also very literal. It takes whatever you say as gospel. Therefore, what it hears when you say, "I hate my job and must find a new one or I will go crazy," is "hate job – go crazy." Very simple, very literal! Now when you say, "I am looking forward to the opportunity of working at a new job that will more stimulating and rewarding," the subconscious hears, "looking forward, opportunity, new job, stimulating and rewarding." Do you see the difference? When you think negative, it is what you get. When you think positive, that is what you get. You are what you think.

Sondra Ray in her book, *The Only Diet There Is*, says that, "An affirmation is a positive thought that you consciously choose to immerse in your consciousness to produce a certain desired result." Thomas L. and Penelope J. Pauley in their book, *I'm Rich Beyond My Wildest Dreams*, state, "Whatever you order, the Subconscious creates. And herein lies the rub – whatever you think, you order."

Let's take something many people think, "I am so fat, I look like a pig, I have to start dieting and going to the gym." What do you think your subconscious is hearing? Yup! "Fat!" "Pig" and "Diet" have never been my favorite words. So, does that encourage you to want to exercise – nope!! What might you say instead? How about, "I see myself slim and healthy at 125 pounds." Well, now you have this really healthy image and it makes going to the gym and exercising a lot more rewarding. What you think is what you get. It is so very simple. You attract what you think.

Once again – YOU ATTRACT WHAT YOU THINK!

> The best of us must sometimes eat our words.
> – JK Rowling from Harry Potter and the Chamber of Secrets

What do you think is the best way to change the way you talk and think? One way is through Positive Affirmations. Positive Affirmations take the self-talk that we all do everyday and change them from negative thought processes into positive energy. It changes negative thinking (or stinkin' thinkin') into positive thinking. And best of all, they work. Here are the easy to follow steps:

- Your affirmation must be in the **present tense** as if it has already happened.
- Your words must be stated in the **positive**. Avoid the use of any negative words such as not, won't, can't, stop, try, etc. All the words must be positive and said in a positive manner.

- They must be **personal**. The words must relate to you and what you want.
- They must be **realistic** to you.
- Your affirmation must have **passion** and be **powerful**. It doesn't matter if you believe it to be true now or not – you simply must state it with passion. The words, though, must resonate within you, vibrate within you, you must feel something to make it real.
- They must be said **out loud**. This way you not only read it but you hear it as well.
- You have to **practice** your affirmation. How often? The more the better, however statistics show that saying it 3 times per day, 10 times each really works. So, for example if your affirmation is: I am beautiful. Then it would be, "I am beautiful," "I am beautiful," "I am beautiful," "I am beautiful," "I am beautiful," "I am beautiful," "I am beautiful," "I am beautiful," "I am beautiful," "I am beautiful," said with passion and out loud.
- **Write the affirmation – do not type it.** Something about writing it also makes it more real. Remember when you were a kid and had to write 100 times, "I will not talk in class?" Well, this is kind of the same thing. Writing it uses another sense that helps to make it more real.
- **Take the affirmations with** you so you can say them whenever, wherever. The best way to have access to the affirmations is to write them on separate 3X5 cards. Have one set on your nightstand to say when getting up in the morning and before going to bed at night. The other set can be slipped into your pocket when getting dressed, stay in the car, in your lunch pail – wherever it will work so you recite them 3 times per day.

- Say them for **21 to 28 days**. The reason for that amount of time is that statistics show that it takes that long to change or make a habit. You want your new affirmation to flow off your lips easily. So if someone were to say to you, "Wow, you look beautiful," you can easily say, "Thank you" because you feel beautiful.
- If your affirmation stops resonating with you, if you don't feel the passion for it, by all means re-write it.
- It's also best to not have more than 5 affirmations that you are working on at one time.

A couple of books that I highly suggest to get more information on affirmations are any books by Louise Hay – *I Can Do It: How to Use Affirmations to Change Your Life* or *You Can Heal Your Life*. I also suggest another book that gives a different idea on affirmations – *The Only Diet There Is* by Sondra Ray.

Sondra Ray from, *The Only Diet There Is*, suggests that you add your name to your affirmations. In other words, it would be something like this: "I, Judith, am now comfortable with achieving all of my goals."

Ray also suggests that:
- Write each affirmation 10 to 20 times on the left side of a piece of paper.
- As you write leave space to the right to write any negative comments that come up as you write the affirmation.
  - In other words, if I were to write my above affirmation, the negative thought that might come up would be – "Sure I am comfortable with that goal – I am such a loser."

- You keep on with the process until you have a neutral response.
- You will want to continue this process until no negative responses come up.

Another suggestion that I really like is that Ray suggests saying them to a friend, and then ask your friend to respond with a "thank you" after each affirmation.

> It's the repetition of affirmations that leads to belief. And once that belief becomes a deep conviction, things begin to happen.
> – Claude M. Bristol

Here are some affirmations to get you started. You can place your name in the affirmation to make it even more powerful.

- I am choosing to change all thoughts that hurt me.
- I am loveable and find love everywhere.
- I am working at the job I enjoy and earning a great salary.
- I am working toward my goals and enjoying the process.
- I am discovering new and wonderful places to visit each weekend.
- I am living in the home of my dreams.
- I am a happy and joyful person.

Affirmations work, and the best way to find out, is to try them. Happy affirming your new self!

> One comes to believe whatever one repeats to oneself sufficiently often, whether the statement be true or false. It comes to be dominating thought in one's mind.
> – Robert Collier

Part XV – Ah, let me write a sonnet of my love for the java bean – let me count the beans? Number One....

> NASA was going to pick a public school teacher to go into space, observe and make a journal about the space flight, and I am a teacher who always dreamed of going up into space.
> – Christa McAuliffe

Journaling is an important part of achieving goals. Through journaling you may explore what you really want – not just what you think you want. Also, journaling releases the imagination to explore aspects of your goal that you may not have thought of. The act of journaling can actually affect your health. From *What's Your Sabotage?* by Alyce Cornyn-Selby "In one study, subjects were asked to spend 20 minutes writing intimately to themselves. When researchers examined blood samples taken after the fourth day, they found evidence of an "enhanced immune response." The trend continued for the following six weeks. Participants who showed the greatest improvement in health were those who wrote about events in their lives! The act of writing can even show up in your blood stream!" This is the power of journaling.

> I can shake off everything if I write;
> my sorrows disappear, my courage is reborn.
> – Anne Frank

Journaling can be as simple or complex as you like. My suggestion is to start simple. Purchase an inexpensive wire bound book from a drug or office supply store. There is no need to spend a lot of money. I personally don't like paper with lines as I feel it boxes me in. But that is just me – you choose what fits you best. Later you may want to invest more money in say a leather bound journal. What is most important is to buy a pen you will enjoy writing with. It needs to be a pen that flows easily. I particularly like pens that will write in almost any direction so that I can be lying down or sitting half up in bed.

You might even choose to use felt markers or crayons. If you use these, be sure to choose paper that does not bleed through or put a piece of cardboard between the pages.

If you have ever seen Frieda Kahlos' journal you will discover the true art of journaling. It is full of imagination, play, thoughts, poetry, words; truly amazing! Once you decide to get more creative with your journal, you can draw, paint, sketch, write poetry, write ideas for an adventure, paste pictures and make small collages.

OK, now you have your journal, open it up and write a dedication to yourself. Then write your name and the date you are starting your journal. In fact, on each new page write the date, time, place, your mood – something to remember where you were and what you were doing when you wrote. I have looked back at my past journals and find this fascinating.

Some suggested writing:

- Things you are grateful for (these may be the same things day after day, page after page.)
- Wins for the day such as staying on your diet or feeling beautiful or ….
- Affirmations
- Write about your day – the good, the bad and the ugly, and the beautiful, too.
- Write about your dreams, your goals
- Write about your past, your future

You might have different journals.
- ◆ Dreams
- ◆ Poetry
- ◆ Money
- ◆ Business
- ◆ Dating, Love, Marriage – What your dream partner will be like
- ◆ Art

Remember, there are no rules for journaling except to do it.

> Journal writing is a voyage to the interior.
> – Christina Baldwin

Part XVI – I not only woke up and smelled the coffee – I actually see the coffee.

Close your eyes. Now visualize your goal. Can you see it? If not, then you are missing a powerful tool toward achieving your goals. Visualization is one of the most important things you will want to do in order to bring your goal to life. It is even better if you get all your senses involved. See it, Feel it, Taste it, Smell it, Hear it. Visualization helps to make it more real. If you can't visualize it, you won't do it.

> Lot's of people wonder….
> Fewer take the time to really think …..
> But I'll be darned, sometimes I think I could count on the fingers of my hand how many actually visualize the life of their dreams, as if their dreams had already come true, every single day, for just 5 or so minutes.
> – the Universe (TUT) TUT.com

In order to get the maximum benefits of goal setting will mean spending time each day visualizing your goals. Really spend time with this. Make it real. It only takes about 5 minutes.

Let me give you an example. Let's say you want to open a donut shop. Do the following:
- Close your eyes and relax. Take a deep breath in and slowly blow it out.
- Picture in your mind that you're standing outside your donut shop. What does it look like? What do you smell? What do you hear?
- Now imagine walking up to the door. Touch the door handle, what does it feel like? Open the door, what sound did you hear. (So far I hear the tinkle of a bell as the door opened and the sound of laughter, and of course, the smell of freshly made donuts. I'm getting hungry for a donut just writing this.)
- Walk in. What does the floor look like? Are there tables and chairs? What does the counter look like? Is there a display case? If so, what is in it? What do you smell? Touch the counter? What does it feel like?

Just in this brief imagery you used nearly every sense: touch, smell, vision, hearing, and for me, taste. This only took a few minutes.

That was so much fun, let's do one more. Let's say you want to weigh 125 pounds. Let's go:
- Close your eyes and relax. Take a deep breath in and slowly blow it out.
- Picture yourself standing in your bathroom. In front of you on the floor is the scale. It is your friend – no anxiety – in fact; you are excited about getting on it and seeing the wonderful results.
- Step onto the scale. The numbers creep up slowly and stop at 125 pounds.

You are elated! You feel beautiful! You feel sexy and healthy and slim.

- Now step off the scale and walk to the full-length mirror. Look at yourself.

  See how beautiful you are at 125 pounds.

- Go to the closet and pick out that dress that you have been dying to wear.
- Put it on.
- Look at yourself in the mirror again.
- Now in your minds eye imagine yourself entering a room with all your friends and loved ones there. Imagine what they are going to say – how good you look, how healthy you look, how happy they are for you.

Now, this may seem silly. How are you going to achieve success just by imagining it? Visualization really works. The mind is a powerful tool.

Part XVII – Do you have a copy of Coffee Lovers Magazine?

> With Shakespeare and poetry, a new world was born. New dreams, new desires, a self-consciousness was born. I desired to know to know myself in terms of the new standards set by these books.
> – Peter Henry Abrahams

Read – read – read and - read. I am not sure where the statistic comes from, but I like it so much that I am going to use it anyway – "20% of the population purchases 80% of the books on goal setting. Successful people have libraries with books on success and self-growth." Now, one very important point that I am going to add is that you read these books. They don't do you any good gathering dust on the shelf. It is actually suggested that you read at least one self-help book a month.

The problem is, there are so many, how do you know which one to choose? I understand this dilemma more than you may realize. I have shelves filled with books. Some I started and said, "ummm, not for me!" and they end up back on the shelf. I suggest going to the library and finding books. If it is a book that you absolutely love, go out and buy it for your personal library. If it is not a book that touches you, you have lost nothing.

I personally purchase books that I really enjoy because I love to mark books up. I write all over them. I highlight, underline, and make comments. So, if I get a book from the library and find myself dying to write all over it, I know I have to go out and purchase it. I am also a great fan of used books stores. In Portland we have many, but one of my favorites is Powell's Books. Amazon.com also has lots of used booksellers. Just make sure that someone like me hasn't had the book first and written all over it.

So, why do self-help books help so much? Because they offer us something to think about and to grow. You do not have to take everything they say as gospel. The best readers are those that really think about what they are reading. Is it worthwhile? Do I really believe in what they are saying? There are going to be books that you love and that will lead you to other self-help books in their genre. And there will be those that you set aside and not finish. That's OK. But read. Help comes from unexpected places.

> A beggar had been sitting by the side of the road for over thirty years. One day a stranger walked by.
> "Spare some change?" mumbled the beggar, mechanically holding out his baseball cap.
> "I have nothing to give you," said the stranger. Then he added, "What's that you are sitting on?" "Nothing," replied the beggar, "Just an old box. I have been sitting on it for as long as I can remember."
> "Ever look inside?" asked the stranger.
> "What's the point? There's nothing in there." "Have a look inside," insisted the stranger. The beggar managed to pry open the lid. With astonishment, disbelief, and elation, he saw the box was filled with gold.
> – Elkhart Tolle from The Power of Now: A Guide to Spiritual Enlightenment

Part XVIII – I can see it all now – life without coffee is impossible.

> I can see clearly now, the rain has gone
> I can see all obstacles in my way
> Gone are the dark clouds that had me blind
> It`s gonna be a bright, bright sunshiny day
> It`s gonna be a bright, bright sunshiny day
> – Johnny Nash

A vision board or collage, is a wonderful way to put your goal altogether. Remember we talked about involving all your senses? Well, having a vision board in front of you everyday is an amazing way to stay focused.

There are no hard and fast rules for creating a Vision Board. However, here are some ideas:

- Buy either foam board or poster board at a stationary store (cardboard boards are $1 at the Dollar Tree or similar stores.)
- If you haven't saved up magazines, then go to Goodwill and other thrift stores for old magazines. You can also check with the library and doctor's offices to see if they have any throw away magazines. You could probably also advertise on Craig's List for old magazines.
- You can also go online and search for photos that might fill your collage needs. Some sites are Google Photos, Flickr Photo Sharing and Yahoo Image Search.
- Put your face onto the face of a models body or in the car you want or in the window of your donut shop.
- You may use glue or if you plan on rearranging, removing, adding to your board, you may want to use thumbtack putty, which rolls up into small balls and makes removing items really easy.
- Scissors, there are a variety of scissors out there to choose from. Many of these make fancy edges that can add some pizzazz to your Vision Board.
- Design your board as you like it. There are a number of ways to design a board. You might want lots of white area, while others like every inch covered.
- I suggest that you have soft or inspirational type music playing while you are doing this. It is best if a Zen like atmosphere is created.

I suggest you create a new Vision Board every 6 months or every time you have a new goal. I create one every January 1st for the New Year.

Another kind of vision board is a Mind Map. This is a method of taking your path toward you goal and creating a map. You can use drawings, pictures from a magazine or the Internet to identify where your baby steps are on the path. This is a fun way to notate your path toward your goal.

> You know a dream is like a river, ever changing as it flows.
> And a dreamer's just a vessel that must follow where it goes.
> Trying to learn from what's behind you and never knowing what's in store makes each day a constant battle just to stay between the shores.
> And I will sail my vessel 'til the river runs dry.
> Like a bird upon the wind, these waters are my sky. I'll never reach my destination if I never try,
> So I will sail my vessel 'til the river runs dry.
> Too many times we stand aside and let the water slip away. To what we put off 'til tomorrow has now become today.
> So don't you sit upon the shore and say you're satisfied.
> Choose to chance the rapids and dare to dance the tides.
> – Garth Brooks song "The River" co-written with Victoria Shaw

Part XIX – Tea is much more fun with two for tea.

> Perfect as the wing of a bird may be, it will never enable the bird to fly if unsupported by the air.
> – Ivan Pavlov

Develop a support team to support you with your goals. To my surprise, most people try to do it alone. I am going to be straight with you here and ask – WHY? Why would you try to do it alone? For the glory? I hope not. Going it alone makes for one thing – a very lonely journey – and the glory in the end is more fun if it is shared. Without a support team it is also much easier to become discouraged and give up! Teamwork is the way to go!

Can you imagine a sporting event without a "rah-rah" team? No way – they love those "rah-rah's" and it keeps the team motivated.

So, who makes a good support team? Pick those that you know you can trust and those with knowledge. My sister Debbie is on my support team. She is great at many things, English grammar being one of them – so I asked her to edit this workbook (you may blame her for any typos or grammatical errors), but I wouldn't ask her to plan a budget for me. For advice on what to invest in for my coaching business, I go to my friend Samuel who provides me with wise advice. If I want to know about marketing or website construction I go to my friend Wendy who is also a spiritual healer – so I get advice on my website and healing all from one visit. If I want a cheering team I go to Leah, Joan, Hazel, Beverlee, Jan, Penny and my many supportive friends. When I am facing a challenge or know that it is time for a kick-in-the-pants, I go to my coach, Joseph, who I trust completely to provide me with just the kick I want and need. Coaches are great that way!! Now your team members can know each other or not. What matters is that you build a team to help support you in your goals. Working it alone takes a lot more time and I have to tell you – you don't know everything. You may know a lot – but I don't know anyone who knows everything.

Imagine someone playing baseball alone – could he or she play all the positions? Well, maybe if he or she was Superman (woman), but generally there is a Lois Lane in the wings ready to help out and cheer Superman on.

According to Thomas L. and Penelope J. Pauley in their book, *I'm Rich Beyond My Wildest Dreams*, "Always ask that only those who are for your highest good be allowed in your life." In other words, you will want to build a team of people who have your best and highest interests at heart. You would not want anyone who was jealous or someone who tended to say things like, "You can't afford that," or in any way puts down your enthusiasm or your ideas. You want to build a support team that is not only honest and forthright with you but is also your cheering fans in the background.

The other good thing about having a support team is that by stating your goal you are half way there. "If you tell somebody else you're going to do it, you're more likely to do it," states Linda Finkle, MCC and CEO of Incedo Group. According to Sean Covey, people are more serious about their goals when they have stated them to others. It is also healthier to have others backing you.

I remember when my son Brian was about four he used to call all his friends, "My buddies." Well, you are going to create "buddies."

Follow these steps to create a support team:
- Make a list of qualities you are looking for in people who will be on your team.
- Now make a list of everyone you know who is supportive or has knowledge you might need that fit the qualities you are looking for. Remember, you may love your mother, but if she tends to put down your ideas or not be completely supportive, you probably do not want her on your team. Or, give her job that she is good at and won't in any way discourage you.
- Now separate them into categories – friends, those with certain knowledge or abilities, those that will cook for you when you haven't time to eat, etc. Have all kinds of categories. For example, your daughter

might be a great one to go to the movie with and relax a little, but she is not the one you might go to if you have concerns about money.

Once you have your team members in their category, then you want to set up the category rules. There have to be rules – for your sake and your team member's sake. Some rules might include:

- How will you meet - in person, by phone or email
- How long the conversation will be and how often. People are more willing to give their time if they know that it will be a maximum of 30 minutes once every 2 weeks. We all have busy schedules and to just arbitrarily say that you will call someone and talk for an undisclosed amount of time, they might not be as willing to be a member of your team.
- Let them know what their duties will be as a member of your team. People like to know what their job duties are. It might be to listen and give feedback, or maybe it will be to just listen, or maybe it is to be a comfortable shoulder to whine or complain on for the allotted period of time – and that they do not need to come up with solutions, just agree along the way. If you don't let your team members know what their duties are and how you want them to respond, they may feel unsure and useless.

As Rhonda Britten stated in her book, Fearless Living, "Your Support Buddies believe in you when you don't believe in yourself. That is the greatest gift of all."

A dwarf standing on the shoulders of a giant may see farther than a giant himself.
– Robert Burton

Three billion people on the face of the earth go to bed hungry every night, but four billion people go to bed every night hungry for a simple word of encouragement and recognition.
– Cavett Robert

Part XX – I drank all the coffee I need and it is time to say adieu – to you and you and you.

The more you praise and celebrate your life, the more there is in life to celebrate.
– Oprah Winfrey

What do you do once you have achieved your goal? Celebrate!!!! OK, now after the celebration is over what do you do? For me, it will be sending this book off to my sister to look for all my typos and grammatical errors.

After the goal is completed it is time to evaluate it.

If it was too simple, too easy, maybe you want to make your next goal more difficult. If the goal took too long and you felt yourself becoming disheartened along the way, consider making your next goal not quite so challenging, or break it down into smaller steps. Remember, if the goal is too hard and takes too long, it is easy to self-sabotage. The idea is to achieve goals with fun and pleasure. Generally speaking, if it isn't fun, you won't see it through to its completion.

If a goal you have set no longer interests you – then let it go. There is no use working on a goal if it no longer suits your needs or your life plan.

Most of all, it is important to watch your capacity. With goal setting it is important to note how much you can "really" get done in a day, a week, a month. Underestimating will leave you with time in which you could have done more. However, in the long run, underestimating is better than overestimating. Underestimating may eliminate the frustration of working against a clock that you arbitrarily set. Keep it simple! Be Kind! Be Gentle! Say "no" when you need to.

And most importantly, write about what you learned. If your goal didn't make it to fruition – that's OK – what did you learn from the experience? What did you gain? Remember, there is no such thing as failure – only learning experiences.

> Stop worrying about the potholes in the road and celebrate the journey!
> – Barbara Hoffman

Part XXI – Next on the list – a good chocolate store – or maybe coffee mocha ice cream!

Remember through this entire book I have talked about celebration and rewards. Well, I saved the best for almost the last. Rewards and Celebration are important to keep you motivated and from self-sabotaging. My suggestion is to have a list of rewards already planned, written down and posted for easy access.

Now I have both short and long term rewards. A short-term reward might be:
- Chocolate (I suggest organic very, very dark chocolate then it is medicinal)
- Going for a walk
- Calling a friend
- Making a nice dinner for yourself with candle light
- Taking a warm bubble bath
- Playing with your pet
- Working in the garden

Keep adding to this list of short-term rewards as you think of them

Long- term rewards are for when you finish a step in your goal or finish the goal itself.

Some ideas are:

- Getting a pedicure and/or manicure or even a spa treatment
- Going out to dinner and a movie with a friend
- Renting a movie and having pizza delivered
- Going for a ride and a picnic in the country
- Going for a hike
- Buying tickets for a play or concert

Again, lots and lots of things to add to this list.

The important thing is to have your rewards and celebrations written down so that you don't have to think about it. Be sure to have friends or support team members ready to celebrate with you.

Part XXII – May I have a little "OMMMM" with my Chai?

> Prayer is when you talk to God; meditation is when you listen to God.
> – Diana Robinson

I am going to add a part that you will not find in most books on Goal Setting. It is in regards to a much higher part of ourselves, which you may wish to address, or not. If this part does not interest you, then by all means, skip on down to the next part. However, if you believe that there is a higher power that intersects into our work here on earth, please read on.

It is funny that talk of a Higher Spirit, God, or Trusted Source is still somewhat taboo in our culture. After living in El Salvador I learned a completely different way of approaching this topic. In El Salvador, God and Faith are just a part of life. When the bombing of the federal buildings in Oklahoma occurred it was easy for me as a teacher in the International School to suggest that we take a moment to pray for the people there. The kids instantly knew what this meant and bowed their heads – each silently saying their own prayer.

Timothy Kelley, as part of his training in "Know Your Purpose," says that the methods to find your purpose include: Prayer, Meditation, Active Imagination, and Dreamwork. Prayer is number one and meditation number two in his list of what is necessary in finding your purpose. Should it be any less for finding and achieving your goal? I don't believe so.

Kelley continues, "You will need to choose a suitable trusted source before using direct access methods (to find your purpose.)" According to Kelley, trusted source takes many different forms "depending on person's belief system." Most of us realize that there are many ways to pray, worship and to speak to our higher self.

One of the newest and most advanced forms of science, quantum physics, has brought together two fields that used to be diametrically apart – science and religion. According to *Pure Inspiration Magazine*, Winter 2008, Effective Prayer page 56, "Quantum physicists describe the universe as consisting of a limitless ether of thought energy which acts like a single, unified mind and which manifests everything in the material world out of nothingness through a process of creative thought." This sounds a lot like God – doesn't it?

Quantum physic scientists have discovered what they call a "universal energy." This energy can be affected by human thought so strongly that it can change the material world.

magazine article, "Some scientists have even found evidence that the way change takes place suggests that the universal energy is trying to give us something to meet our expectations. Science is now coming into harmony with the spiritual teachers who have been telling us for many centuries that we can change ourselves and even the world around us by raising our consciousness and attuning ourselves to the love of God through affirmations, positive thinking, faith, mediation, and creative prayer."

So, if God, Spirit, or whatever you wish to call it exists, then it makes perfect sense to include prayer and meditation as part of your goal work. How you do this is up to you – I am not going to teach you how to pray, meditate or to prescribe a certain method. There are others who are more versed in this than I. However, I use prayer and meditation and find it truly does help. You have all my blessings.

> ...essentially a period of meditation and prayer, of spiritual recuperation, during which the believer must strive to make the necessary readjustments in his inner life, and to refresh and reinvigorate the spiritual forces latent in his soul.
> – Baha'u'llah

Sources

Beardshall, Thomas, (2008, Winter). Effective Prayer. Pure Inspiration #6, 56-60.

Beck, Martha. (2001). Finding Your Own North Star. New York: Three Rivers Press.

Britten, Rhonda. (2001). Fearless Living. New York: The Berkley Publishing Group.

Buaxwmi, Karen, (2007, Winter). 10 Steps to Get What You Really Want Out of Life. Successful Living, Volume 1 Issue 2, 20 - 25.

Cornyn-Selby, Alyce. (1999). What's Your Sabotage?. Oregon: Beynch Press Publishing Company.

Kelley, Timothy. (2003-2008). Know Your Purpose. (Participant Manual, February 28-March2, 2008, Petaluma, CA).

McGraw, Phillip C. (2001). Self Matters. New York: Simon & Schuster Source.

Pauley, Thomas L., Penelope J. (1999). I'm Rich Beyond My Wildest Dreams. California: RichDreams Publishing.

Ray, Sondra (1981). The Only Diet There Is. California: Celestial Arts.

True Wealth Community. (2007). Blueprinting Living Your Life by Design…Not by Chance!. Page 11. www.joinpeak.com

All inspirational quotes used in this book were from quote websites on the Internet – available free of charge.

www.WiseHeartCoaching.com

Worksheets

Worksheets

Now it is time to go to the worksheets. I will supply the instructions for each sheet. Please follow the directions as stated as this will produce the best results.

I wish you the very best in working and achieving your goals. Please feel free to contact me if you have any questions. I would also love to hear of your successes. You may reach me at my website, www.WiseHeartCoaching.com where you will find a fill-in form that will be sent directly to me.

Statistic (from where is an unknown) but of interest none the less:

> Researchers tracked fifty people beginning at age seven and reevaluated them every seven years until age 35. Surprisingly, all subjects found work that was related to interests they had demonstrated between the ages of seven and fourteen. Although most of them had discarded or strayed from those interests in early adulthood, virtually all had found their way back to their childhood aspirations by age 35.

Worksheet List

A suggestion is to **Make Copies** of the sheets so you will be able to use the originals over and over. Do remember that any copying for sale or to use in a class needs to be approved with the author or Judith Auslander first. **Note:** Worksheet page numbers include a **"W"**.

Pages 1-3	Questions to go over to see if you are ready for goal setting
Page 4	Words Have Power
Page 5	Life Value Prioritization Grid – Instructions
Page 6	Life Value Prioritization Grid
Page 7	Values Sheet – Instructions
Page 8	Values Sheet
Page 9	Life Value Prioritization Grid – Blank – Instructions
Page 10	Life Value Prioritization Grid - Blank
Page 11	Balance Wheel – Instructions
Page 12	Balance Wheel
Page 13	Blank Balance Wheel
Page 14	Balance Wheel Assessment
Page 15	Bucket List 101 Goals – Instructions
Page 16	Bucket List 101 Goals
Page 17	Dreams vs. Goals
Page 18	Know Thyself
Page 19	Journeling: Dreams Into Goals
Page 20	What is Your Masterful Plan
Page 21	Life Strategies – Instructions
Page 22 – 23	Life Strategies for Balance
Page 24	The Gap in Life Strategies Balance
Page 25	Goal Setting Development
Page 26	Where Have You Been
Page 27	Where Will You Be in Five Years
Page 28	Reverse Planning
Page 29	My List of Incompletes
Page 30-34	Inspirational Goal Quotes
Page 35	The Happy Dance

GOAL SETTING AND ACHIEVEMENT

In this personal assessment, circle the number which comes closest to representing how true the statement is for you. This assessment helps discover your current goal-setting capabilities. (1=less true; 3=more true)

1. I have a sincere and forthright interest in getting to know myself.	1	2	3
2. I have a formula for success to experience a high level of achievement.	1	2	3
3. I have the knowledge, skills, and abilities to build a purposeful life.	1	2	3
4. I have an incredibly strong commitment to achieving my goals.	1	2	3
5. I have a specific, clear, and direct plan for my future.	1	2	3
6. I know how to be self-motivated and resourceful.	1	2	3
7. I have a deep appreciation for all my efforts and accomplishments.	1	2	3
8. I have no fear, because I feel competent and comfortable being creative and assertive on my journey toward achieving my goals.	1	2	3
9. I am aware of how I'm changing and what I'm learning to achieve my goals, as well as maturing as a person.	1	2	3
10. I know how to accentuate the positive when things get challenging.	1	2	3
11. I guide and direct my actions to get closer to my goals.	1	2	3
12. I specifically know what my goals are and I can already visualize myself achieving them.	1	2	3
13. I let go of my past setbacks to move forward to accomplish new goals.	1	2	3
14. I am constantly reviewing my progress, results, and desired purpose.	1	2	3
15. I write out my daily, monthly, yearly, and five-year goals so I can keep on track with my life mission.	1	2	3
16. I know who I am, so my values and goals are in alignment.	1	2	3
17. I automatically know when to change direction and apply a contingency plan when I'm not reaching my goals.	1	2	3
18. I listen fully and carefully to those who support my goal efforts.	1	2	3
19. I achieve a goal then cross it out and write another goal to keep the process going and to continue living an empowered life.	1	2	3
20. I know how to coach others to achieve their goals.	1	2	3

Total: _____

SCORING:

50–60 You are living on purpose—congratulations! Highly effective at goal setting and achieving. Keep it up. Recommend coaching others to live a purposeful and productive life.

36–49 Highly capable of being purposeful. Recommend ongoing learning and studying goal-setting strategies, as well as working with a performance coach.

20–35 At this time, skills are limited. Recommend support, training, and/or coaching.

SELF-OBSERVATION

Reflect then specifically answer each question. Use additional sheets of paper if necessary.

1. What is your family's history of goal setting and achieving. Focus on how your family expressed what they wanted and how they got it.

2. Briefly describe your earliest memory of setting a goal. Did you achieve it? How did you feel afterward?

3. What has been your greatest personal accomplishment thus far? How did you focus on achieving this goal? What did it feel like after your goal was achieved?

4. What have you learned about your goal setting skills and abilities? How do you handle setbacks when you don't get what you want or set out to achieve?

_____
_____
_____
_____
_____
_____
_____
_____

5. What has stopped you from setting goals throughout your life?

_____
_____
_____
_____
_____
_____
_____
_____

SHOULD, CAN'T, NEED, TRY, BUT

Words have power. Here a few very powerful words to avoid.

SHOULD: We "should" ourselves a lot. Others make "should" statements to us. Should is a judgment. When we "should" ourselves we set ourselves up for not feeling very good. I see a finger wagging in front of my nose. Let's eliminate "shoulding" ourselves, others, or allowing others to "should" us. If someone "should's" you, suggest they reframe their words - that you would prefer not being "should" on.

CAN'T: The word "can't" is disempowering. It removes all our power. The thing we can't say or do now is overpowering us. Instead, how about the words, "I choose?"

NEED: We think we "need" this or "need" that. Need is a sign of desperation and fear. How about instead stating we would like this or that or it might be nice to have this. Need is limiting. Without the item or thing we think we need we are not whole or complete.

TRY: This is a huge one. "I will try to do this or that." What "try" does is allow us to fail. "Well, I tried!" Try means you are really NOT doing it. Instead, how about, "I can do that," "I will work on that," or statements that show positive action steps. Or as Yoda in Star Wars said, "Do or do not... there is no try."

BUT: This is a great one. "OK, but…." What "but" does is discount. If there is one word to discontinue using it is "but." Imagine, I love you, but ……!!

Life Value Prioritization Grid Instructions

1. Before starting, look the sheet over.
2. Please note that you will be working vertically up and down – not across.
3. Next note the different values written in the box below.
4. The first step will be to compare value number one to value number two. In other words – compare number 1 Achievement to number 2 Work. Circle either number 1 or number 2 in the pyramid as to which has more value to you. Do not think about this too long. Make a choice and move on.
5. Next you will be comparing number 1 Achievement to number 3 Adventure and then comparing number 2 Work to number 3 Adventure.
6. After that you will be comparing number 1 Achievement to number 4 Personal Freedom and number 2 Work to number 4 Personal Freedom and last number 3 Adventure to number 4 Personal Freedom.

    There is no definition of any of the words – it is what they mean to you. Work as quickly as possible so that you do not spend a lot of time analyzing. Go with the gut.
7. Continue with the method of moving down each row until you complete the entire chart.
8. Now you count how many times you circled number 1, Achievement, and write that number in the box next to Achievement.
9. Now do the same for number 2 – count all the times you circled it. Remember to look down and up as the number switches places. The most a number may be circled is 19 times.
10. Now pick out your top 5 values and write them on the sheet under "Top 5 Values." You may have ties.
11. Now pick out your values that that scored the lowest and write them on the "Bottom 3 Values."
12. **I KEPT NOTES OF MY FEELINGS DURING THIS EXERCISE AND I NOTICED CERTAIN WORDS AFFECTED ME IN CERTAIN WAYS. WHAT DID YOU NOTICE?**

LIFE VALUES PRIORITIZATION GRID
(from What Color is Your Parachute by Richard Nelson Bolles and Whistle While you Work by Richard J Leider)

Pairwise comparison grid: for each pair of values (numbered 1–20), circle the one you prefer.

1,2	1,3	1,4	1,5	1,6	1,7	1,8	1,9	1,10	1,11	1,12	1,13	1,14	1,15	1,16	1,17	1,18	1,19	1,20
	2,3	2,4	2,5	2,6	2,7	2,8	2,9	2,10	2,11	2,12	2,13	2,14	2,15	2,16	2,17	2,18	2,19	2,20
		3,4	3,5	3,6	3,7	3,8	3,9	3,10	3,11	3,12	3,13	3,14	3,15	3,16	3,17	3,18	3,19	3,20
			4,5	4,6	4,7	4,8	4,9	4,10	4,11	4,12	4,13	4,14	4,15	4,16	4,17	4,18	4,19	4,20
				5,6	5,7	5,8	5,9	5,10	5,11	5,12	5,13	5,14	5,15	5,16	5,17	5,18	5,19	5,20
					6,7	6,8	6,9	6,10	6,11	6,12	6,13	6,14	6,15	6,16	6,17	6,18	6,19	6,20
						7,8	7,9	7,10	7,11	7,12	7,13	7,14	7,15	7,16	7,17	7,18	7,19	7,20
							8,9	8,10	8,11	8,12	8,13	8,14	8,15	8,16	8,17	8,18	8,19	8,20
								9,10	9,11	9,12	9,13	9,14	9,15	9,16	9,17	9,18	9,19	9,20
									10,11	10,12	10,13	10,14	10,15	10,16	10,17	10,18	10,19	10,20
										11,12	11,13	11,14	11,15	11,16	11,17	11,18	11,19	11,20
											12,13	12,14	12,15	12,16	12,17	12,18	12,19	12,20
												13,14	13,15	13,16	13,17	13,18	13,19	13,20
													14,15	14,16	14,17	14,18	14,19	14,20
														15,16	15,17	15,18	15,19	15,20
															16,17	16,18	16,19	16,20
																17,18	17,19	17,20
																	18,19	18,20
																		19,20

Values

1. Achievement (sense of accomplishment)
2. Work (paying your own way)
3. Adventure (explorations, risks, excitement, etc.)
4. Personal Freedom (independence, making own choices, etc)
5. Authenticity (being frank and genuinely myself)
6. Expertness (being good at something important to me)
7. Service (contribution to satisfaction of others)
8. Leadership (having influence and authority)
9. Money (plenty of money for things I want.)
10. Spirituality (meaning to life, religious beliefs, need for something greater than self, etc.)
11. Physical health (attractiveness and vitality)
12. Emotional Health (ability to cope well with life and respond to inner or outer conflict in a reasonable way)
13. Meaningful Work (relevant and purposeful job)
14. Affection (warmth, caring, giving and receiving love)
15. Pleasure (enjoyment, satisfaction, fun)
16. Wisdom (mature understanding, insight)
17. Family (happy and contented living situation)
18. Recognition (being well-known, prestige)
19. Security (having a secure and stable future)
20. Self-Growth (continuing exploration and development of self)

Top 5 Values
1. _____
2. _____
3. _____
4. _____
5. _____

Bottom 3 values
1. _____
2. _____
3. _____

www.WiseHeartCoaching.com   W6

Values Sheet Instructions

There are actually many ways to use this Values Sheet. You may design your own method. This is one way.

1. Look at each column and circle 5 values in each column. This will give you 20 values.
2. Now from those 20 values bring it down to 10.
3. From those 10 bring it down to your top 5 values.

VALUES

Accuracy	Education	Intelligence	Security
Achievement	Effectiveness	Kindness	Self-actualization
Adaptability	Energy	Knowledge	Self-control
Adventure	Encouragement	Leadership	Self-denial
Affection	Enjoyment	Learning	Sensibility
Alertness	Enterprise	Love	Simplicity
Ambition	Enthusiasm	Loyalty	Sincerity
Assertiveness	Excellence	Maturity	Skillfulness
Authenticity	Faith	Meticulousness	Sociability
Balance	Fitness	Modesty	Status
Beauty	Flexibility	Nurturance	Strength
Boldness	Focus	Optimism	Success
Broad-mindedness	Foresight	Organization	Sympathy
Calmness	Forgiveness	Originality	Tact
Capability	Freedom	Patience	Talent
Care	Friendliness	Peace	Teamwork
Career	Fulfillment	Perseverance	Thankfulness
Clear-thinking	Generosity	Personal mastery	Thoroughness
Compassion	Gentleness	Persistence	Tolerance
Competence	Good attitude	Playfulness	Tranquility
Confidence	Growth	Politeness	Trustworthiness
Conscientiousness	Hard work	Practicality	Understanding
Consideration	Happiness	Precision	Uniqueness
Contentment	Health	Professionalism	Value
Contribution	Helpfulness	Progress	Versatility
Cooperation	Honesty	Prosperity	Victory
Courage	Hope	Punctuality	Vigor
Creativity	Humility	Purposefulness	Warmth
Customer service	Humor	Quality	Willpower
Dependability	Imagination	Quickness	Wisdom
Determination	Impartiality	Resourcefulness	Wit
Diligence	Independence	Respect	Youthfulness
Discipline	Innovation	Responsibility	Zeal
Dynamism	Integrity	Satisfaction	

Life Values Prioritization Grid – Blank

Here is another way that you can find your top 5 values.

1. Pick out 20 values from the Values Page.
2. List them in the blank 20 slots on the blank Prioritization Grid
3. Now perform the same elimination process as you did with the filled in Prioritization Grid. If you have not filled out the other Prioritization Grid yet, just follow the directions on Page W5.

Other ways to use the Blank Prioritization Grid

You can list all the values you want in a:
- relationship
- career or job change
- car
- home or apartment
- roommate

The list is endless – think of anything you want to know what your top needs or values are and just fill it in.

If you want to use only 10 or 15 slots – you may do that as well.

LIFE VALUES PRIORITIZATION GRID
(from What Color is Your Parachute by Richard Nelson Bolles and Whistle While you Work by Richard J Leider)

	2	3	4	5	6	7	8	9	10	11	12	13	14	15	16	17	18	19	20
1	1,2	1,3	1,4	1,5	1,6	1,7	1,8	1,9	1,10	1,11	1,12	1,13	1,14	1,15	1,16	1,17	1,18	1,19	1,20
2		2,3	2,4	2,5	2,6	2,7	2,8	2,9	2,10	2,11	2,12	2,13	2,14	2,15	2,16	2,17	2,18	2,19	2,20
3			3,4	3,5	3,6	3,7	3,8	3,9	3,10	3,11	3,12	3,13	3,14	3,15	3,16	3,17	3,18	3,19	3,20
4				4,5	4,6	4,7	4,8	4,9	4,10	4,11	4,12	4,13	4,14	4,15	4,16	4,17	4,18	4,19	4,20
5					5,6	5,7	5,8	5,9	5,10	5,11	5,12	5,13	5,14	5,15	5,16	5,17	5,18	5,19	5,20
6						6,7	6,8	6,9	6,10	6,11	6,12	6,13	6,14	6,15	6,16	6,17	6,18	6,19	6,20
7							7,8	7,9	7,10	7,11	7,12	7,13	7,14	7,15	7,16	7,17	7,18	7,19	7,20
8								8,9	8,10	8,11	8,12	8,13	8,14	8,15	8,16	8,17	8,18	8,19	8,20
9									9,10	9,11	9,12	9,13	9,14	9,15	9,16	9,17	9,18	9,19	9,20
10										10,11	10,12	10,13	10,14	10,15	10,16	10,17	10,18	10,19	10,20
11											11,12	11,13	11,14	11,15	11,16	11,17	11,18	11,19	11,20
12												12,13	12,14	12,15	12,16	12,17	12,18	12,19	12,20
13													13,14	13,15	13,16	13,17	13,18	13,19	13,20
14														14,15	14,16	14,17	14,18	14,19	14,20
15															15,16	15,17	15,18	15,19	15,20
16																16,17	16,18	16,19	16,20
17																	17,18	17,19	17,20
18																		18,19	18,20
19																			19,20

Top 5 Values
1. _____
2. _____
3. _____
4. _____
5. _____

Bottom 3 values
1. _____
2. _____
3. _____

1. _____
2. _____
3. _____
4. _____
5. _____
6. _____
7. _____
8. _____
9. _____
10. _____
11. _____
12. _____
13. _____
14. _____
15. _____
16. _____
17. _____
18. _____
19. _____
20. _____

www.WiseHeartCoaching.com

Balance Wheel Instructions

The **Balance Wheel** is a very important part of goal setting as it determines where you might want to bring your life into more balance and where you may want to set some goals.

Before starting, read the instructions that are written on the bottom of the page of the Balance Wheel. Basically, looking at each part as a slice of the pie, place a dot in the center of the pie piece where your life is in relation to that value. Say for example "Mental" (and the definition is whatever that means to you) if you feel that your mental needs are not being met, you would put your dot very near the hub or center of the wheel as a zero. Moving out of the circle, if you mental needs were totally being met, you might put it on the rim at a 10. Any place in between would be from 1 to 9.

Do this for each pie slice. Then just follow the directions.

For the **Blank Balance Wheel**, you can put anything on the outside that you might want to. This is totally optional and up to you.

For the **Balance Wheel Assessment sheet**, the first thing you are going to want to do is make 5 copies of it. One for 6 months, another for 1 year, another for 2 years, another for 5 years and another for 10 years. This is where you list how you plan on bringing your life back into balance. Will your goals change in a year or more? More than likely – but this gives you goals to work toward.

The Life Balance Components

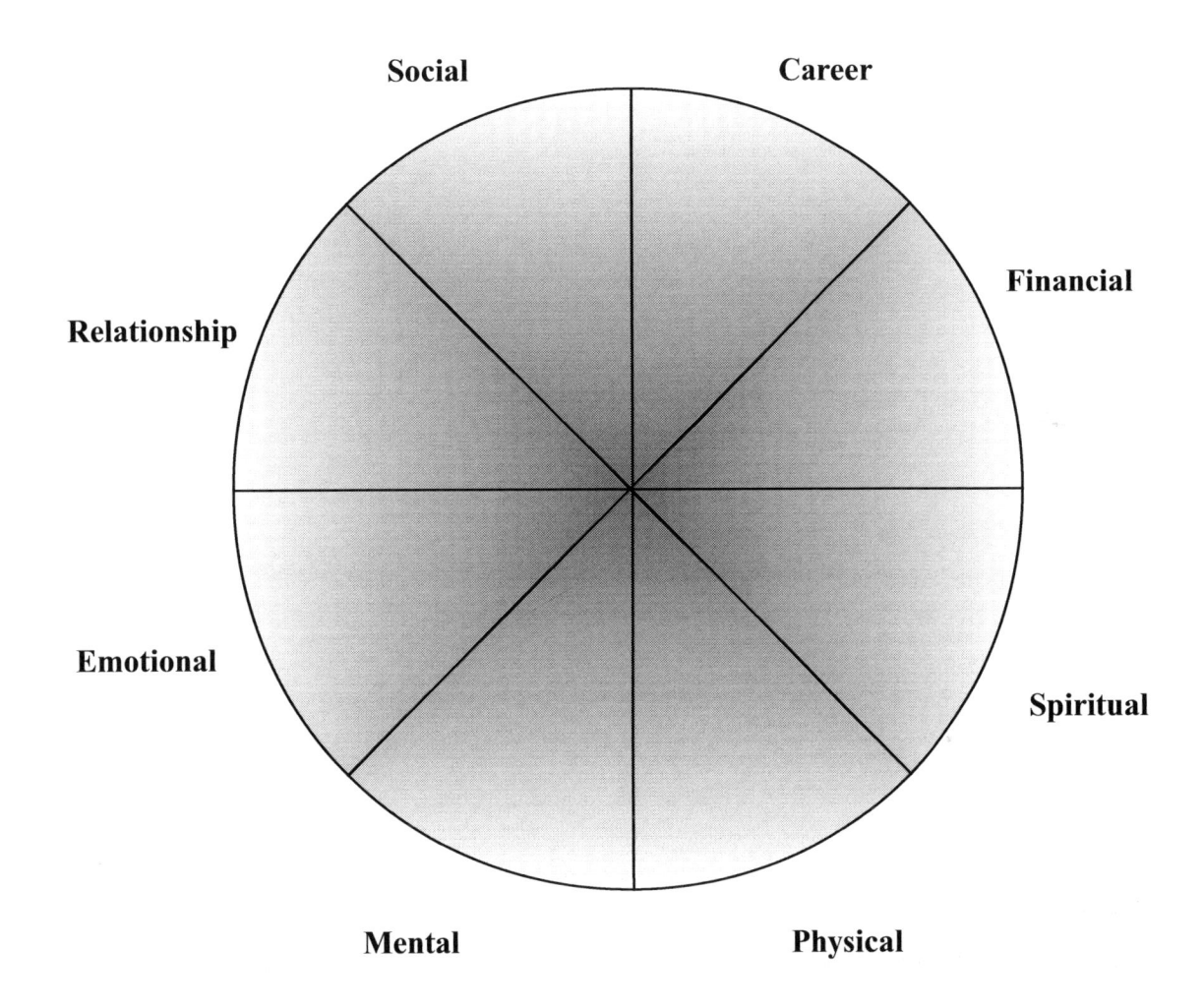

Labels around the wheel (clockwise from top): Social, Career, Financial, Spiritual, Physical, Mental, Emotional, Relationship

The eight sections in the Wheel of Life represent balance. Regarding the center of the wheel as 0 and where you are not meeting these needs and the outer edge as 10 where your needs are being met, rank your level of satisfaction with each life area by placing a dot in that area. Now draw a line to connect the dots and to create a new outer edge. How bumpy would the ride be if this were a real wheel?

www.WiseHeartCoaching.com W12

The Life Balance Components - Blank

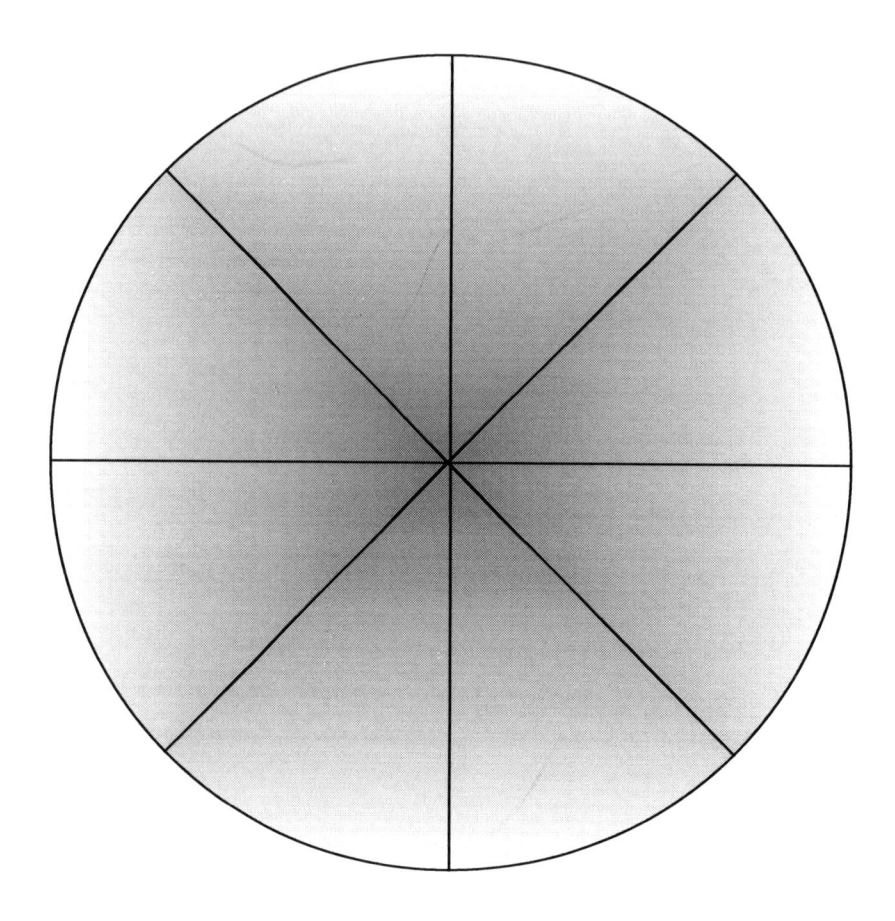

The eight sections in the Wheel of Life represent balance. Label this wheel with eight priorities in your job or in your life. Upon completion of the labeling, score your sense of satisfaction with your priorities on a scale from 0 to 10, with the center of the wheel as 0 and the outer edge as 10. Identify one or two scores that you want to impact immediately. What actions will you take? When will you take these actions? What support do you require to ensure that the actions occur?

www.WiseHeartCoaching.com

BALANCE WHEEL ASSESSMENT

What goals will you fulfill in the following areas of the Balance Wheel of your life in the next 6 months, year, 2 years, 5 years, 10 years? <u>Copy this sheet and fill it out for each of the 5 year spans.</u>

Relationship/Family
1.
2.
3.
4.

Spiritual
1.
2.
3.
4.

Physical/Health
1.
2.
3.
4.

Mental
1.
2.
3.
4.

Emotional
1.
2.
3.
4.

Social
1.
2.
3.
4.

Financial
1.
2.
3.
4.

Job/Career
1.
2.
3.
4.

www.WiseHeartCoaching.com

Bucket List Instructions

This is a fun list that you fill out as you go along.

- ◆ It is not something that you do in one sitting.

- ◆ It is a list you keep adding to.

- ◆ From it may come some new goals to work on.

- ◆ Circle the ones you really want to accomplish.

- ◆ Which ones do you want to accomplish in one year, two years, five years, ten years?

Bucket List
List 101 – Then Circle your top 10 highest-priority goals.

Easiest way to fill this out is about 33 each of

To Be - a pilot, To Do - Learn to play the piano, To Have - a home

1.	35.	69.
2.	36.	70.
3.	37.	71.
4.	38.	72.
5.	39.	73.
6.	40.	74.
7.	41.	75.
8.	42.	76.
9.	43.	77.
10.	44.	78.
11.	45.	79.
12.	46.	80.
13.	47.	81.
14.	48.	82.
15.	49.	83.
16.	50.	84.
17.	51.	85.
18.	52.	86.
19.	53.	87.
20.	54.	88.
21.	55.	89.
22.	56.	90.
23.	57.	91.
24.	58.	92.
25.	59.	93.
26.	60.	94.
27.	61.	95.
28.	62.	96.
29.	63.	97.
30.	64.	98.
31.	65.	99.
32.	66.	100.
33.	67.	101.
34	68.	

www.WiseHeartCoaching.com

Dreams Versus Goals

Dreams plant the seed that grows into a goal

A dream is a:
- Hope
- Desire
- Wish

A strongly <u>desired</u> goal or purpose

A goal is:
- Specific
- An action
- Concrete
- Achievable

The end toward which <u>effort</u> is directed

Examples

Dream: To be a professional athlete.

Goal: Workout daily. Go out for two sports, get good grades, and get a sports scholarship to a college within two years.

Dream: To start a pet grooming business.

Goal: Investigate an area where a pet grooming business is needed. Find various means of funding the business. Open doors in 6 months.

Take a dream and make it into a goal.

Dream: _____

_____

Goal: _____

_____

Dream: _____

_____

Goal: _____

_____

W17 www.WiseHeartCoaching.com

Know Thyself!

Before you can achieve your goals you must first know yourself. What are your strengths and weaknesses? Where can you improve?

Identity
- The distinguishing character or personality of an individual
- Observing yourself—personally and professionally
- Modifying yourself and progressing toward growth

Personal Inventory
Make an observation about your life. Compile an inventory of your gifts, and your personal and professional strengths. Compile your areas to strengthen.

GIFTS/STRENGTHS	AREAS TO IMPROVE
Personal:	Personal:
▪	▪
▪	▪
▪	▪
Professional:	Professional:
▪	▪
▪	▪
▪	▪

Action Steps in areas to improve

- ◆
- ◆
- ◆
- ◆

Journaling – Dreams Into Goals!

What dreams or goals did you have as a child for your life?

What would you do for free?

If you knew you only had a month left to live, what would you do?

Imagine you have accomplished your greatest achievement, what would it be?

If you could leave one mark on the world before you leave it, what would it be?

Under <u>no</u> condition would I ever…

Do 5 Things Every Day Toward Your Goal!!!!

WHAT IS YOUR MASTERFUL PLAN?

Be a Masterful Dreamer

Every master is a master of dreaming. Dream big, and then plan your future. Take your dream, make it a goal, go even further and then live out your destiny.

What is your dream for the future? Write about it and visualize it in your minds eye.

List two things you believe your world and the world around you needs today.

1.

2.

List two ways you can contribute to make great changes happen.

1.

2.

Describe the legacy you believe you will leave to the world:

My Life Strategies for Balance Instructions

This is a **3-part** exercise.

The <u>first part</u> is **My Life Strategies Balance** sheet which is 2 pages long. In this part you will check off all the ones that are true under each section. You may add anything that is true for you that was not mentioned in the bottom. Or you may write something that was not listed that you wish were true in that area.

<u>Next</u> you are going to move to **The Gap in Life Strategies Balance.** On this sheet you will write all the things that you did not mark as true on the **My Life Strategies Balance** sheet that you would **want to be true**.

<u>Last</u> is the **Goal Setting Development** Sheet. This sheet is pretty self-explanatory. You will want to use one of these sheets for each one of your baby steps. So make lots of copies.

MY LIFE STRATEGIES FOR BALANCE

1. Check each true (for you) item. 2. Transfer any "not true" items that you want to integrate into your life to… The Gap in Life Strategy Balance (following page)

Career/Lifework

1. ___ I am enjoying a career that is aligned with my vision and purpose.
2. ___ My work environment is nurturing.
3. ___ I have the certifications, degrees, and credentials for my profession.
4. ___ I have close business associates.
5. ___ I devote one hour to reviewing and goal setting each week.
6. ___ I am at the top of my pay scale.
7. ___ I share the passion of my work with others.
8. ___ I continue to read and take continued education courses for further career growth.
9. ___ I keep my desk and office organized and meet my deadlines.
10. ___ I set a positive example by being ethical and following a rule of conduct.
11. ___ I am creative, energetic, and success-minded.
12. ___ I put enough time into my work and work smarter, not harder.
13. ___ I am a professional and people reap benefits from me.
14. ___ I have a business/marketing plan and follow it often.
15. ___ I have a contract with a publisher for my book.
16. ___ I love what I do.
17. ___ I do informational interviews with those who wish to do what I do.
18. ___ I dress for success.
19. ___ I have a professional coach to guide my growth in my life work.
20. ___ (other:_____)

Health/Well-Being

1. ___ I exercise 3 to 4 times per week.
2. ___ I get enough sleep every night.
3. ___ I take vitamins daily.
4. ___ I have a healthy diet; I know what my body needs and I make sure I get it.
5. ___ I drink a minimum of 8 glasses of water daily.
6. ___ I maintain a high standard of personal grooming.
7. ___ I have health-minded associates in my life.
8. ___ I keep my stress level low and pace myself.
9. ___ I seek spiritual growth through daily affirmations.
10. ___ My family shares my value for healthy living—we practice healthy eating and exercise.
11. ___ I get a medical checkup yearly and see my dentist every six months.
12. ___ I educate myself (books, magazines, etc.) about health, fitness, and healthful living.
13. ___ I am going to live long into my senior years and enjoy good health.
14. ___ I am at my ideal weight and feel comfortable about my age.
15. ___ I enjoy humor and laughing, and take time for hobbies, travel, etc.
16. ___ I understand my feelings and manage my anger appropriately.
17. ___ I get up early and have a half hour of personal time just for me.
18. ___ I am aware of my negative habits and am constantly working on my personal growth.
19. ___ I get assistance from counseling, coaching, or education professionals, when needed.
20. ___ (other:_____)

www.WiseHeartCoaching.com

Prosperity/Finances

1. ____ I save at least 10% of my monthly income.
2. ____ I contribute at least 10% of my income monthly to charity.
3. ____ I have at least four months of cash available for emergencies.
4. ____ I have a secure retirement plan and I'm setting goals for a happy senior life.
5. ____ I stay well informed about money and finances.
6. ____ I have little to no debt and spend within my means.
7. ____ I have a financial record-keeping method to trace my cash flow.
8. ____ I have a financial advisor and am informed about tax deductions.
9. ____ I know how to create wealth and prosperity and I am wise with money.
10. ____ I have a manageable house mortgage, and dependable, safe transportation.
11. ____ I model myself after those who have done well financially.
12. ____ I provide a high quality of life for my family and myself.
13. ____ I have medical, dental, vision, and life insurance plans.
14. ____ I have a network of friends and associates who are financially responsible.
15. ____ I have a healthy belief system about money and finances.
16. ____ I am a generous person.
17. ____ I teach my family about financial wisdom.
18. ____ My credit is good.
19. ____ My will and estate planning are complete; I am leaving an inheritance I feel good about.
20. ____ (other:_____)

Lifestyle/Relationships

1. ____ I have a healthy relationship with my spouse/partner/significant other.
2. ____ I have a healthy support group of family, extended family, and friends.
3. ____ My home is a warm and welcoming place.
4. ____ I am authentic and share warm smiles with those around me.
5. ____ I spend quality time with my spouse/partner/significant other doing fun activities.
6. ____ I communicate effectively, positively, and assertively and get great results.
7. ____ I have patience and understanding, and I support others.
8. ____ I express my gratitude and appreciation.
9. ____ I attend workshops, listen to tapes, read, and do whatever it takes to grow personally.
10. ____ I live my life with integrity and maturity and tell the truth.
11. ____ I ask for what I want and need without hesitation.
12. ____ I give at least 2 to 4 hours per month to community service.
13. ____ I am emotionally, mentally, physically and spiritually balanced.
14. ____ I am a person who is joyful, happy, and loves life.
15. ____ I do not live in the past; I know how to put closure to it.
16. ____ I have set my boundaries with others.
17. ____ I read to my family and encourage education in my home.
18. ____ I forgive others and ask forgiveness as well.
19. ____ I live my life according to how I want to be remembered.
20. ____ (other:_____)

THE GAP IN LIFE STRATEGY BALANCE

Write in any statements that were <u>not</u> marked "true" on your Life Strategy Balance Assessment that you would like to manifest in your life.
Transfer your desired goals to the Step-by-Step Goal Setting sheet and then move toward action.

Career/Lifework
-
-
-
-
-
-

Health/Well-Being
-
-
-
-
-
-

Prosperity/Finances
-
-
-
-
-
-

Lifestyle/Relationships
-
-
-
-

_____ **(Your choice here)**
-
-
-
-

GOAL SETTING DEVELOPMENT

Please keep this as an original and make copies.

Life Balance Components:
- ❏ Emotional ❏ Personal Growth ❏ Physical ❏ Spiritual ❏ Organization
- ❏ Financial ❏ Career ❏ Social/Play ❏ Relationship ❏ Mental

Specific Goal: _____

Specific Baby Step Goal: _____

Desired Date of Achievement: _____

Priority Action Step: _____

Small Purposeful Steps

Task	Step #	By When	✔

EXTRA GOAL SETTING DEVELOPMENT

<u>**Please keep this as an original and make copies**</u>.

Life Balance Components:
- ❏ Emotional ❏ Personal Growth ❏ Physical ❏ Spiritual ❏ Organization
- ❏ Financial ❏ Career ❏ Social/Play ❏ Relationship ❏ Mental

Specific Goal: _____

Specific Baby Step Goal: _____

Desired Date of Achievement: _____

Priority Action Step: _____

Small Purposeful Steps

Task	Step #	By When	✓

www.WiseHeartCoaching.com

Where Have You Been?
Where Are You Now?

Examine the following areas of your life.

Career/Lifework
Year Ago: _____
Present: _____

Mentally
Year Ago: _____
Present: _____

Spiritually
Year Ago: _____
Present: _____

Emotionally
Year Ago: _____
Present: _____

Physically
Year Ago: _____
Present: _____

Relationships/Lifestyle
Year Ago: _____
Present: _____

Socially
Year Ago: _____
Present: _____

Financially
Year Ago: _____
Present: _____

www.WiseHeartCoaching.com

WHERE WILL YOU BE IN FIVE YEARS?

Be specific.

CAREER/LIFEWORK _____
_____
_____

MENTALLY _____
_____
_____

SPIRITUALLY _____
_____
_____

EMOTIONALLY _____
_____
_____

PHYSICALLY _____
_____
_____

RELATIONSHIPS/LIFESTYLE _____
_____
_____

SOCIALLY _____
_____
_____

FINANCIALLY _____
_____
_____

REVERSE PLANNING

Here is another way to make goals fun. Do it in reverse!

Take a huge sheet of paper so you have lots of room.

- Write at the top your ultimate goal of what you want to achieve.

- State everything about it – every little detail. Who is going to assist? Who is going to handle what details? What items will you need? Who will help you get what you need? Everything!

- Then work backwards slowly of how you are going to reach this ultimate goal. Step by step by step - see the entire picture of how you are going to get from the end to the beginning.

Go for it!!! This takes the pressure out of starting small – eventually you will get there.

Be with spirit!! And have fun!

My List of Incompletes

To Do & Ta Dah's	Delegate It	Hire It	Do it in 10 Min.	Discard It	A-P Day	When	Done

Legend: **Delegate It** – Find someone to get it done **Hire It** – Hire someone to get it done **Do It in 10** – Those things that bug you that can be done in 10 minutes or less – just get them done **Discard It** – Find those things that haven't any real use and take it to Goodwill or have a garage sale **A-P Day** – (From FlyLady.com) Anti Procrastination Day **When** – Decide a date to have it done

Created by Rena Tuttle, Lighthouse Coaching, LLC

www.WiseHeartCoaching.com

A Select Collection of Goal Quotes

Louis Pasteur

Let me tell you the secret that has led me to my goal: my strength lies solely in my tenacity.

Les Brown

Life takes on meaning when you become motivated, set goals and charge after them in an unstoppable manner.

You cannot expect to achieve new goals or move beyond your present circumstances unless you change.

You are never too old to set another goal or to dream a new dream.

Your goals are the road maps that guide you and show you what is possible for your life.

One of the most essential things you need to do for yourself is to choose a goal that is important to you. Perfection does not exist; you can always do better and you can always grow.

Arnold H. Glasgow

Make your life a mission-not an intermission.

Aristotle

Man is a goal-seeking animal. His life only has meaning if he is reaching out and striving for his goals.

Elbert Hubbard

Many people fail in life, not for lack of ability or brains or even courage but simply because they have never organized their energies around a goal.

Helen Keller

Many persons have the wrong idea of what constitutes true happiness. It is not attained through self-gratification but through fidelity to a worthy purpose.

Cecil B. DeMille

Most of us serve our ideals by fits and starts. The person who makes a success of living is one who sees his goal steadily and aims for it unswervingly. That's dedication.

Ronald Reagan

My philosophy of life is that if we make up our mind what we are going to make of our lives, then work hard toward that goal, we never lose - somehow we win out.

Denis Waitley

No man or woman is an island. To exist just for yourself is meaningless. You can achieve the most satisfaction when you feel related to some greater purpose in life, something greater than yourself.

Edgar A. Guest

You are the person who has to decide. Whether you'll do it or toss it aside; you are the person who makes up your mind. Whether you'll lead or will linger behind. Whether you'll try for the goal that's afar. Or just be contented to stay where you are.

Mark Victor Hansen

You control your future, your destiny. What you think about comes about. By recording your dreams and goals on paper, you set in motion the process of becoming the person you most want to be. Put your future in good hands - your own.

Tracy Brinkmann

You must have an aim, a vision, a goal. For the man sailing through life with no destination or "port-of- call', every wind is the wrong wind.

Ralph Marston

Your goals, minus your doubts, equal your reality.

George Shinn

There is no such thing as a self-made man. You will reach your goals only with the help of others.

Scott Reed

This one step - choosing a goal and sticking to it - changes everything.

Orison Swett Marden

We advance on our journey only when we face our goal, when we are confident and believe we are going to win out.

Maxwell Maltz

We are built to conquer environment, solve problems, achieve goals, and we find no real satisfaction or happiness in life without obstacles to conquer and goals to achieve.

Zig Ziglar

What you get by achieving your goals is not as important as what you become by achieving your goals.

Remember, what you get by reaching your destination isn't nearly as important as what you become by reaching your goals - what you will become is the winner you were born to be! Outstanding people have one thing in common: an absolute sense of mission.

What you **get** by achieving your goals is not as important as what you **become** by achieving your goals.

Napoleon Hill

When defeat comes, accept it as a signal that your plans are not sound, rebuild those plans, and set sail once more toward your coveted goal.

Greg Anderson

When we are motivated by goals that have deep meaning, by dreams that need completion, by pure love that needs expressing -- then we truly live life.

Richard Bach

Here is a test to find out whether your mission in life is complete. If you're alive, it isn't.

Og Mandino

I am here for a purpose and that purpose is to grow into a mountain, not to shrink to a grain of sand. Henceforth will I apply all my efforts to become the highest mountain of all and I will strain my potential until it cries for mercy.

Mary Lou Retton

I'm very determined and stubborn. There's a desire in me that makes me want to do more and more, and to do it right. Each one of us has a fire in our heart for something. It's our goal in life to find it and to keep it.

Mary O'Connor

It's not so much how busy you are, but why you are busy. The bee is praised. The mosquito is swatted.

Jim Rohn

Pity the man who inherits a million and isn't a millionaire. Here's what would be pitiful, if your income grew and you didn't.

J.C. Penney

Give me a stock clerk with a goal and I'll give you a man who will make history. Give me a man with no goals and I'll give you a stock clerk.

Maxine Hong Kingston

To me success means effectiveness in the world, that I am able to carry my ideas and values into the world -- that I am able to change it in positive ways.

Michelangelo

The greatest danger for most of us is not that our aim is too high and we miss it, but that it is too low and we reach it.

Robert H. Schuller

Goals are not only absolutely necessary to motivate us. They are essential to really keep us alive.

Anatole France

To accomplish great things, we must not only act, but also dream; not only plan, but also believe.

Victoria Holtz

Your role in achieving your goal must be giving your all. Involve yourself whole: with your heart, your mind and your soul.

Judith Auslander

A goal is the key that starts the engine of your future.

Ayn Rand in *Atlas Shrugged*

"To me, there is only one form of human depravity - the man without a purpose."

I am adding The Happy Dance to the worksheets because I believe it is a great motivator – and you can't help but be "happy" when you do it.

This is from TUT and whenever I am feeling down – I do …

THE HAPPY DANCE

Arms up and out, half bent, hands just above head level, facing your peeps (that's your eyes) waving in a circular fashion. Subtly sway to the left, then to the right. Keep with it, back and forth. Don't stop waving. Now mix in a gentle bob, up and down... That's right, good...

Now add a little, "Whoo-hooooo, Whoo-hoooo....." as you sway.

Perfect.

Just 5 seconds of this happy dance, just 5 seconds, even when feeling blue, will always make you smile. Your smile will lift your spirits. Your spirits will summon ancient friends. And your friends will raise you higher into the light.

Works every time.

This has been a public service announcement brought to you by.... *The Universe*

TUT.com

Judith Auslander, MA

It has been along the Road Less Traveled that Judith found her way to becoming a Life Coach. Not one to take the short, direct path, she has accumulated many life experiences along the way.

Following her graduation in 1990 from The Evergreen State College in Olympia Washington, she moved to El Salvador where she was determined to learn more about life and people. "I discovered what it is like to be a Stranger in a Strange Land, and I learned to communicate in an entirely new way - and to be quiet and listen."

Upon her return to the United States in 1996, she attended Pacific University and received her Masters Degree in Teaching.

It was through taking advantage of life experiences that she learned about The Centre For Coach Training in Portland Oregon where she took classes and graduated as a Certified Professional Life Coach and a part of the International Coach Federation.

www.WiseHeartCoaching.com

In 2012, Judith returned to university to attain a second masters – Masters of Arts in Interdisciplinary Studies with a focus in Gerontology. In Summer, 2013, she graduated as a Sage-ing Leader through Sage-ing® International.

In May 2014 Judith will be taking hypnotherapy training through The Wellness Center in Issaquah, Washington. She will open up her practice as a hypnotherapist in Fall, 2014.

She holds certifications as an Core Value Index Practitioner, EFT Practitioner, Cognitive Rehab Therapist, and Crisis and Peer Counselor.

"I am a "Baby Boomer" and enjoy all the fun and challenges that come with growing older."

Judith is available for speaking engagements and to facilitate workshops. She promises that everyone will have a fun time, as she believes that "laughter is the best medicine on the market."

www.WiseHeartCoaching.com

What Is Coaching?

A Professional Coach can help you:

- ♦ Discover who you are and what really motivates you!

- ♦ Create the life you want to follow your passions, priorities, and talents!

- ♦ Set and achieve proactive, powerful goals rather than just reacting to life!

- ♦ Achieve the goals you really want and do so on your terms!

- ♦ Breakout of self-defeating, self-sabotaging behaviors!

- ♦ Gain a true supportive partner throughout the process to assure that you achieve your goals!

- ♦ Celebrate your victories and enjoy the wonderful rewards from achieving your goals!

- ♦ Unleash the Powers within you, to accomplish more than you ever thought possible!

How is Coaching Different from Counseling?

Coaching is a different and separate profession from counseling or psychotherapy in that it focuses on the present and on what you can do to create the future you want - NOW!!! Coaching involves clarifying your values, your goals, your purpose and mission in life. As your Life Coach I will facilitate this process by asking provocative questions, offering honest feedback and inspiring you with new ideas, concepts, strategies and frameworks that help reorient you around success as YOU define it. Throughout the process, I will offer a supportive environment by championing you when things are moving forward and

www.WiseHeartCoaching.com

respecting and challenging you when progress gets stalled. I will be there as your friend, mentor, supporter - and most importantly - treat you with honesty and respect.

The International Coach Federation (ICF) Definition of Coaching

Professional Coaching is an ongoing professional relationship that helps people produce extraordinary results in their lives, careers, businesses or organizations. Through the process of coaching, clients deepen their learning, improve their performance, and enhance their quality of life. In each meeting, the client chooses the focus of conversation, while the coach listens and contributes observations and questions. This interaction creates clarity and moves the client into action. Coaching accelerates the client's progress by providing greater focus and awareness of choice. Coaching concentrates on where clients are now and what they are willing to do to get where they want to be in the future. ICF member coaches recognize that results are a matter of the client's intentions, choices and actions, supported by the coach's efforts and application of the coaching process. If coaching sounds like something that would add quality to your life, please contact me for a free consultation.

Would you like a business that has inspired employees?

I help inspire employees and management toward higher achievement through team building. What does this mean to the business owner? It means happier employees. What do happier employees mean? It means that your employees look forward to coming to work each day. They take pride in the work that they do. It also means less time off for illness and injuries. It also means that your trained employees will <u>not</u> be looking elsewhere for employment. This means less money spent in hiring and training new workers. Contact me today to find out if Team Building will benefit your company.

www.WiseHeartCoaching.com

When management and employees are working toward the same goals, when an employee feels needed, listened to and relied on, and that they are a part of the company, they are more engaged in what they are doing. I would be happy to coach your businesses to help build team support to work together toward both company and personal goals.

Is Group Coaching for you?

Group coaching works great and costs less. Check out when my next group coaching class takes place by visiting my website WiseHeartCoaching.com. There you will find a form where you can provide me with a phone number so may call you and discuss if group coaching would work for you.

Individual Coaching might be for you!

Various programs are available depending on your need. Programs for 4 to 12 weeks are available. Visit my website, WiseHeartCoaching.com and send me an email. I will call you and we can discuss what would work best for you.

I look forward to working with you toward a better tomorrow.
Does it get any better than that?

Judith Auslander, MA, PCC

Thank You

As a thank you for purchasing *The Power of Goal Setting – Transforming Thoughts Into Action!* - Wise Heart Coaching is offering you **$75 off** a coaching program.

Just go to WiseHeartCoaching.com and hit "Contact Me" and send me a message stating that you would like to take advantage of the **$75 off** a coaching session.

Or you may clip this and send it to:
Wise Heart Coaching
PO Box 934
Beaverton, OR 97075-0934

Name _____

Email Address _____ Phone _____

Order More

To Order More Copies of The Power of Goal Setting – Transforming Thoughts Into Action!, please visit WiseHeartCoaching.com. You can find links to order more hard copies from Create Space or you download the e- book version and print it yourself.

Thank you so much for believing in the Power of Goal Setting.

www.WiseHeartCoaching.com

Send me a message

I would love to hear your comments about the book. Please fill in the form below or visit my website at WiseHeartCoaching.com, All comments are appreciated and listened to. Also let me know of any grammatical errors or typos. Thank you.

After reading your book, "The Power of Goal Setting – Transforming Thoughts Into Action!" I would like to comment on:

- how it changed my life in _____ way
- I found the following errors
- or what ever you would like to share

_____

_____

_____

_____

_____

_____

_____

Name _____ Phone # _____

Address _____ City _____ State ____ Zip _____

Email Address _____

Please mail your comment to:

Wise Heart Coaching
P O Box 934
Beaverton, OR 97075-0934

---

www.WiseHeartCoaching.com

Made in the USA
Charleston, SC
24 January 2016